BRUNTSFIELD PIRATES

THE CHILDREN OF BRUNTSFIELD PRIMARY

This book is dedicated to Miss Dobie and Miss MacKinnon with many thanks for their years of commitment to the pupils of Bruntsfield Primary School.

FOREWORD

Children and their families come to Bruntsfield Primary School from all over the world. Indeed, that is one of the things which makes this a wonderful school to be a part of. Some children are with us for only a part of their primary school years before heading off to new places. This book is filled with stories created by our pupils of crews of pirate children setting off to distant places in search of something, but then ultimately returning to Bruntsfield Bay to share the treasure they have found with its inhabitants.

   I would like to offer a huge thanks to Ramy, who yet again has inspired our pupils to write their stories and who has volunteered so much of his time to make this book out of these stories. Thanks too to Jay and Ady for their work on this project.

   This book is a testament to the time our pupils spend with one another here at Bruntsfield Primary School, however long that may be. All our pupils, of course, inevitably leave the school and go off on the next part of their journeys. These stories are about the times they have spent together collaborating, playing and having fun. At school we learn not only from books but also from one another, from their experiences and from looking at how they see the world. This book celebrates that diversity.

Lesley Lamond
   Depute Head
   Bruntsfield Primary School

A SCHOOL FOR PIRATES

My son pointed to the page and shouted out, "Confused!"

He looked at me with searching eyes. "Confused," he repeated.

I wanted to say something back, but a sudden and uncompromising lump had lodged itself in the back of my throat and as I fought back a tear, I simply nodded, acknowledging his word: "Confused."

Let me explain...

I don't often tear up when my son is confused. Generally, his confusion leads to chaos, us being late to some 'unlateable' event and me apologising to onlookers as we run about in my futile attempt to regain lost time.

But this 'confused' filled me with pride.

You see, last year I volunteered at Bruntsfield Primary to bring about a book I'm sure will be studied by distant future generations: *The Brunstfield Superheroes*.

I'm sure many of you have been forced to read it at bedtime. For that, I'm sorry.

In fact, this aforementioned, "Confused" was, indeed, my own bedtime horror, reading his P2C superhero story: TITLE

I started reading it and before I finished the first paragraph, he told me to skip to the last page.

The last page? You mean, the climax? And ruin this riveting story? I am a writer... that's sacrilege!

No way, no how, no sir!

Then he hit me with that look he's perfected over the last seven years of his life. You know the one: big pleading eyes, slightly furrowed brow, an almost imperceptible lip quiver.

Sighing, I skipped ahead and read these words:

'OOOFFF,' said the children.

Bob the cat-dog crawled out of Romeo Rupeo's neck. He looked queasy

and confused...

My son hit the book and cried out, "Confused! That's my word!" His excitement was tangible.

Huh?

"That's my word," he continued. "When we were working on the book, I said, 'Confused.' And look, there it is!"

He was so proud. He was a writer. He contributed a 'word' to the story... 'Confused.'

That one word made the whole project worth it... at least for me.

As you prepare to delve into this year's book, *Bruntsfield Pirates*, I hope you unearth your child's word buried somewhere within this tome. That is the true treasure of this endeavour, no matter how painfully written (and toilet-humour-driven) these stories may be.

Cheers from very proud, happy and oft confused dad...

Ramy Habeeb

June 6th, 2023

P5A

1

WHAT IS "DUCK" IN JAPANESE?

P5A

Treasure
The final frontier
These are the voyages of the pirate ship T.T.B.T.T.
Its ultimate mission
To plunder strange new lands
To seek new riches
And new wealthy civilizations
To boldly go where no pirate has pillaged before.

A foghorn wailed in the distance as a signal to all ships
"All crews on deck! All crews on deck!" came the order from Pirate King Grrrhooley.

Captain Dirbey jumped to attention and shouted, "Main Deck! Main Deck!"

The pirate crew of *The Titanic Before The Titanic*, otherwise known as T.T.B.T.T., ran to their alphabetical line positions, ready to listen to their orders.

"Move out the way!" grunted Keigo.

"Get to your own spot. You're always in the wrong place!" complained Nilay.

"Shhh! Shhh!" hushed Theo. "We won't know what to do, and Captain Dirbey will be seriously annoyed if we don't hear the Pirate King's orders!"

Olivia muttered, "Someone will be walking the plank before the day is out!"

"I don't want it to be me!" responded Emilie.

"Ahem! You have been selected to sail to a far-flung destination, where you must recover specific important and priceless treasures. You must also return them safely to Bruntsfield Bay to meet the rest of the fleet. Your ships' captains will be given your sailing orders, maps and lists of provisions. You can of course take your pet!"

And with that, Pirate King Grrrhooley disappeared back into his Pirate Palace overlooking the bay and the foghorn whined to a stop.

Captain Dirbey stepped forward with the rolled-up manuscript of sailing orders to share with the crew.

"Clap once if you hear my voice!"

Clap, the crew replied.

"Clap twice if you hear my voice!"

Clap, clap, clap! the crew replied.

"Oh, for goodness' sake, who doesn't know what two is? Don't bother answering—I don't really want to know!" Captain Dirbey continued, "Anyway—that's more like it! Right—these are our orders! We are on our way to... Japan! And the treasure can be found at Mt Fuji!

"All the jobs have been given out. Fern, you know what you are responsible for—make sure we have enough food on board for all the crew and for Bloopy... and chocolate... lots of chocolate... it's going to be a long voyage!

"Fresh water is a necessity—and of course Fanta for me! Get that sorted, Lucia!

"Skye, weapons—cannons, pistols, cutlasses, catapults and pea shooters! You know the usual things!

"Maps, lots of maps... Disneyland, Caribbean Sea, Duddingston Loch, Water of Leith, Union Canal... oh... and a route to Japan!"

"Can we take our reading books, Captain?" asked Holly

"Of course you can—only suitable pirate topics though! *Treasure Island*, *Piratepaedia*, *Pirate Stew*, *The Legend of Captain Crow's Teeth*... You know the ones I mean!

"Right, you horrible lot—get moving!" the captain shouted as she went to her cabin.

Excitedly the crew ran off to their different jobs. The chatter between the different pirates was deafening.

"Have you sailed to Japan before? What is it like?" asked Ruaridh.

Jude exclaimed, "I'm really excited!"

"I'm worried about how I'm going to tell my mum!" said Anna.

"How long will we be gone?" asked Finn.

"What do we need to pack?" asked Farah. "Can I take my stuffed panda?"

"Who is going to look after Bloopy? We must make sure we have him cared for!" Alexandra cried.

"Who or what is this Bloopy that everyone is talking about?" asked Claire.

"Bloopy is not a what... Bloopy is an axolotl, and he's the ship pet," replied Zoya.

"He's invaluable! He's great in a crisis," agreed Jack.

"Get on with it, you lot! We're going to be the last ones to leave if we're not careful," nagged Kody.

It didn't take long for the fleet to be ready to leave. Everyone could feel the excitement in the air as they waited for the tide to turn, and they could leave Bruntsfield Bay and head for where their treasures lay...

Pirate King Grrrhooley watched with pride from his Pirate Palace balcony as his ships left the bay. *T.T.B.T.T.* was accompanied by her sister ships *T.O.B.T.O.* (*The Olympic Before The Olympic*) and *T.B.B.T.B.* (*The Britannic Before The Britannic*). Once in open water, they headed their separate ways.

All was fine on board for many days as they made their way eastwards. They had their sails up and were making good speed.

"Land ahoy," screeched First Mate Awesome from the crow's nest. "Land ahoy!"

"I thought it would take longer?" questioned Captain Dirbey. "We shouldn't be anywhere near land yet!"

"That's not land!" cried Second Mate Sandie Sails.

The crew shouted at once, "That's the Loch Ness Monster! AAARGGGGHH! What on earth is she doing here?"

"Can a monster no' go on her holidays without some numpty making a fuss!" bellowed Nessie in a very unfriendly way. "And you can keep away from my snacks too!" she said, waving a large lettuce and belching loudly. "BuuuUUUrrrPPp!"

"Arrgggh!" screamed Captain Dirbey. "One whiff of that and —" Too late, she had passed out cold!

"You've wiped out our captain!" Second Mate Sandie Sails screamed at the monster. "She reacts really, really badly to lettuce!"

"We've lost so many cooks because of that! Keelhauled all of them!" added Brodie.

"I've had enough o' you lot! I'm no' interested in your lunch problem. I'm on my way for an All-Ye-Can-Eat buffet!" replied the monster. "Get oot my way!"

And with a flick of her colossal tail, she sent an ENORMOUS wave into the side of the ship. The pirates fell to the deck like berries from a bush. No sooner had they got to their feet than they realised someone fairly important was missing...

"Man overboard!" came the cry from Jiqing, "Actually, captain overboard!"

"Captain Dirbey's in the water!"

"Meep! Meep!" cried a distraught Bloopy, watching his favourite person floundering in the waves.

"Drop the dinghy over the side, Captain Dirbey can get herself to a safe port. We can't change our mission, and the monster has taken up enough of our time. We must keep moving eastward," ordered First Mate Awesome.

The dinghy was launched, and Captain Dirbey floated off with her Fanta and chocolate to keep her going. Nessie continued her Mediterranean holiday, and *T.T.B.T.T.* set course for Yokohama...

T.T.B.T.T. continued its leisurely cruise through the Suez Canal and into the Indian Ocean. The weather grew warmer and warmer, and everyone was feeling very positive about their mission. They saw exciting islands and interesting countries from the deck as they sailed by. They wanted to visit them but knew they had to keep moving eastward as quickly as they could.

The ship's crew took turns on watch and looking after Bloopy, who was still very upset that he had lost Captain Dirbey. They made sure that he had fresh clean water in his tank and caught exotic fish from the ship for his carnivorous diet. Some tried to entertain him as best they could to take his mind of his loss with an almost endless supply of *Peppa Pig* videos. They played games on deck when it was quiet. Books were read and re-read and swapped between them. They loved a sea shanty and created some of their own to keep themselves busy.

One quiet night, as they neared their destination, the crew were sleeping soundly in their hammocks, except for Isolde and Gregor, who were being kept awake by Ahmed's heavy snoring. They were secretly reading under their covers, then realised they weren't the only ones awake. They spotted Natalie sneaking through the door and up on deck.

"Where do you think Natalie is going?" asked Emily.

"I don't know, let's follow her," replied Gregor.

They hopped out of their hammocks as quietly as they could and silently tiptoed upstairs to the deck to see where Natalie had gone.

"Do you hear something?" Natalie whispered. "I heard a movement up here."

"Nah, it's probably just the waves or the rats or Ahmed snoring! I'm sure there's nothing... Let's get back to bed," said Gregor.

"Argghhh! That's not rats. That's CAPTAIN BLOOD-DUCK!" screamed Isolde.

Captain Blood-Duck, the most vicious and villainous pirate on the seas, had just leapt over the side of his ship, *The Rusty Bucket*, and onto the *T.T.B.T.T.*, quickly followed by his crew and his pink lion, Fluffy Paws. He raised his cutlass, and with a blood-curdling cry launched himself at Natalie and turned her into a purple rubber duck!

"That cutlass is lethal," screamed Isolde. "Captain Blood-Duck can turn anything into a rubber duck and make it harmless in a fight!"

"He transforms his enemies, steals all their treasure and sends them floating on the tide," Gregor added.

"Arrrrghhhh!" he swiped his cutlass again, and this time each of them were turned into blue and pink dotty rubber ducks. He picked them up and threw them over the side into Yokohama harbour. Before the rest of the crew could get up to the main deck, Captain Blood-Duck's crew had searched the ship, stolen what they could get their hands on and Fluffy Paws appeared with the treasure map clamped between his very, very, sharp teeth. The lightning attack was over—Blood-Duck and his crew had disappeared, but so had the map!

At first light, First Mate Awesome woke the crew. "We are now approaching Yogurthama!"

"It's *Yokohama*!" corrected Second Mate Sandie Sails. "Get your facts straight!" Everyone was in a very cranky mood that morning. The map was gone, the rest of Captain Dirbey's chocolate and Fanta was gone and so were Bloopy's *Peppa Pig* movies! They had at least been able to rescue all the rubber duck crew from the attack the night before.

"Let's look at the positives," said Osso.

"We have safely arrived in Yokohama... and we can get fresh supplies for the rest of our journey," said Eli.

"But we don't know where we're going from here," cried Lottie

"Oh yes we do! Bloopy memorised the map!" Oscar said with a grin.

"We need to get on the bullet train to Mt Fuji and then look for the treasure when we get there," responded Alisha.

"We'll have to keep a look out for Captain Blood-Duck's crew though—they know our destination, and they won't give up if they know there is treasure at the end."

"Well stop your chattering and let's get moving!" said Second Mate Sandie Sails.

The crew raced to the train station and First Mate Awesome bought tickets for them all—return tickets to Mount Fuji. They pushed and shoved their way onto the train—arguing as usual. Many of the pirates were grumbling about being on land—it wasn't their thing! Four crew members were posted to keep an eye out for Captain Blood-Duck, and the rest tried to settle down. Although the journey was very smooth and very fast, they felt uneasy.

Jude got out his accordion and started to play a well-known tune to cheer them up and make them feel at ease. The crew started to sing their own version of "What Shall We Do with the Drunken Sailor?" that matched their mood.

What shall we do with Captain Blood-Duck?
What shall we do with Captain Blood-Duck?
What shall we do with Captain Blood-Duck?
Early in the morning.

Chuck him overboard with his cutlass
 Chuck him overboard with his cutlass
 Chuck him overboard with his cutlass
 Early in the morning.

What shall we do with Captain Blood-Duck?
 What shall we do with Captain Blood-Duck?
 What shall we do with Captain Blood-Duck?
 Early in the morning.

Get that lion off our main deck
 Get that lion off our main deck
 Get that lion off our main deck
 Early in the morning.

Feeling much happier, the crew began to enjoy the bullet train journey, but not for long...

"What on earth is that coming towards us?" shouted Nilay, one of the lookouts.

"It's huge and getting closer by the second. Arrrggghhh!!!" screamed Theo.

"It's an enormous wave.... a tsunami!" stuttered Olivia.

"That's not a normal tsunami!" said Emilie.

"Is there such a thing as a normal tsunami?" asked Fern.

"Well, it's not water!" Lucia shouted, "What is it? It's multi coloured for starters... it's RUBBER DUCKS!"

"Captain Blood-Duck is trying to derail us with his rubber ducks!" said Skye.

Luckily for the crew, the bullet train was travelling at such a speed and was so aerodynamic that it ploughed through the wave of ducks. It looked like a rainbow had appeared over them.

They all took a deep breath and prepared for their final destination. Mt Fuji.

"There it is. Mount Fuji!" shouted Holly. "At last!"

The mountain was huge and almost a perfect cone shape.

"It's still an active volcano!" said Ruaridh.

"Well, I hope it doesn't erupt while we're here!" replied Anna.

"I think we should be safe," said Finn, "although we are now in the Ring of Fire."

"Oh no!" Farah exclaimed.

"What?" said Alexandra

"Look who is here ahead of us!" Farah continued. "Captain Blood-Duck and Fluffy Paws."

"Where're his crew? I can't see them," Alexandra replied.

Captain Blood-Duck and his lion were already digging at the foot of the mountain and hadn't seen the *T.T.B.T.T.* crew arriving.

"They must be in the right spot.... They have the map!" whispered Claire.

Bloopy from his travel tank meeped. "Bloopy agrees—that's where the treasure is!"

The crew army crawled towards the villains, holding their cutlasses in their teeth and hoping they wouldn't be seen. Suddenly, there was a rumble, and the earth around then began to shake. Luckily for the crew, they were safe lying on the ground.

"Earthquake!" shouted Second Mate Sandie Sails.

The ground opened up in front of Captain Blood-Duck and

a treasure chest appeared, as if by magic... exactly where he had been digging! Quickly, Captain Blood-Duck picked up the chest, spun around and tried to escape with the treasure. The earth was still shaking, and because of his wooden leg he lost his balance. Fluffy Paws was terrified by the earthquake and threw himself at his captain. The chest flew from Captain Blood-Duck's hands towards the amazed and silent pirate crew.

"Quick Zoya, go and grab it before he has a chance to attack us!" shouted First Mate Awesome.

Everything seemed to happen in slow motion. Zoya grabbed the chest as Captain Blood-Duck and Fluffy Paws were thrown backwards into the hole created by the earthquake and disappeared without a trace!

The earth stopped shaking, and apart from a few boulders and trees being uprooted, it looked the same as they had first seen it... but with no Captain Blood-Duck and no pink lion! The crew didn't need a minute to think before they ran as fast as they could back to the bullet train station.

"Let's get out of here!" shouted Jack

"Home! We're going home!" Kody cried, jumping up and down. "We've got the treasure—mission accomplished!"

When they returned to the ship, Natalie, Gregor and Isolde had been turned back into themselves—the cutlass' magic had gone too!

The journey home to Bruntsfield Bay was uneventful. The weather was kind, they had plenty of new provisions on board and Bloopy was very pleased with the sushi. The crew relaxed, knowing they weren't going to cross paths with Captain Blood-Duck and his villainous crew ever again!

Captain Dirbey was waiting for them and congratulated them for getting the treasure, returning safely with her ship and defeating Captain Blood-Duck.

"Well done, *T.T.B.T.T.*! You have returned with your treasure! Celebrations are in store for all the returning ships!" exclaimed

Pirate King Grrrhooley. The treasure chest was handed over and the delighted crew went to celebrate their safe and successful homecoming.

"Just out of interest... did anyone ever find out what 'duck' is in Japanese?" asked Brodie as a little yellow rubber duck floated by.

P2C

2

IN SEARCH FOR THE SPECIAL TREASURE

P2C

Captain Ahoy was playing beachball with her P2C pirate crew in Bruntsfield Primary School. Captain Ahoy had a stripy red jumper and big golden earrings that jangled about when she spoke. First Mate One Eye had just scored a goal when the P2C pirate crew heard a strange sound.

"Squeak, squeak!"

It was a squirrel! It had a furry body and a fluffy, golden tail. The P2C pirate crew were surprised and amazed.

"Is that a talking squirrel?" asked Second Mate Err Me Matey.

"Yes, I'm a magical talking squirrel. My name is Squeaky and Pirate King Grrrhooley has sent me to give you all a special secret mission. You need to go and find some very special treasure. He gave me this old map. Let's look at the map and go hunt for the treasure!"

The squirrel then cast a magic spell. Suddenly a giant pirate ship appeared. It had a skull and crossbones flag. The sails were red with skulls. It had lots of canons and loads of different compartments for the P2C pirate crew to sleep in. The ship was called *Squidhead*. Captain Ahoy looked at the map and spotted a glowing X at the North Pole. Squeaky the Squirrel suggested that they should start by going to the North Pole.

After a long journey, Captain Ahoy and her P2C pirate crew finally made it there.

There was lots of snow and ice and it was very, very cold. Suddenly, they saw something in the distance. It was a big man with a long white beard and a red woolly hat. He had a sleigh that was being pulled by polar bears and reindeers.

"It's Santa!" shouted First Mate One Eye. "Let's ask him if he knows where the treasure is!"

Santa said he didn't know where the treasure was, but that his polar bears had heard a lemming talking about some treasure in New York City. He gave them some chocolate as a present to keep them going.

The P2C pirate crew hopped back into their ship and sailed to New York. In New York, they saw lots of skyscrapers. It was very busy and smelly. They even had to dodge a wrecking ball. They were lost and confused, so Squeaky the Squirrel asked a friendly looking skunk if he had seen any treasure.

"No," chirped the skunk, "but I did hear a colourful bird saying something about some golden treasure that was hidden deep in the Amazon jungle!"

The pirate crew were very happy to leave smelly New York and set sail for the Amazon jungle. They sailed up the huge Amazon River, passing fierce alligators. They anchored the ship and marched down the gangplank.

"Watch out for these piranhas!" shouted Squeaky the Squirrel as the water churned and frothed beneath them.

High above them in the canopy flew squawking parrot families and colourful butterflies. As they crept through the thick green undergrowth, they spotted sleepy sloths, jumping jaguars and poisonous red dart frogs. Suddenly, a banana hit Captain Ahoy on the head!

"Owwww. Ouch! What was that?!" she shouted angrily.

"Look, some cheeky monkeys are throwing bananas at us," cried First Mate One Eye.

The monkeys screeched, "Get out of our jungle."

The captain and the pirate crew threw some pineapples back at the monkeys and ran back to *Squidhead*.

"Come on!" shouted Captain Ahoy. "I don't think the treasure is here, let's go try somewhere else."

Next, the pirate ship sailed to the African savanna. Here they met a very tall giraffe family chomping on some green leaves. The pirates asked the giraffes if knew anything about treasure. The giraffes told them all about a bad pirate who had also been looking for treasure.

"His name is Captain Milk Thirsty Ahoy. His nose is very big, and he attacks people by putting his finger on one of his nostrils and squirting milk at them. This makes people go to sleep so he can steal all their things! He stole all our golden flowers! He is a bad pirate!"

"Do you know where he went?" asked Captain Ahoy.

The tallest giraffe looked down at the pirate and said, "He was going to Australia to find some extra special treasure under a rainbow-coloured sandcastle. I hope you find the treasure before he does!"

So Captain Ahoy, Squeaky the Squirrel and the rest of the crew set sail for Australia. They landed on a beautiful sandy beach. On the beach they saw some footprints. A little crab with a colourful shell scuttled towards them.

"Are you looking for a pirate with a big nose who squirts milk? He went that way. Just follow the footprints. I heard him talking about some treasure that is hidden under a big rainbow sandcastle."

Captain Ahoy and her P2C pirate crew thanked the little crab with the colourful shell and followed the footsteps. It was very hot and dry. They walked past some palm trees, some spiky plants and lots of pink shells. They crossed over a little crystal-coloured river, and there right in front of them was a giant rainbow sandcastle. And digging next to it was an ugly pirate with a very big nose. He had a small evil looking octopus sitting on his shoulder. Just then, the evil octopus spotted them and began to chatter. "Milk alert, Milk alert."

Captain Milk Thirsty Ahoy dropped his spade, turned round and with an evil grin, put a finger over one nostril. Milk began spraying out, and Captain Ahoy, First Mate One Eye, Second Mate Err Me Matey and the P2C crew all fell fast asleep. They started to snore.

The octopus gave an evil laugh and waved its tentacles. They didn't notice Squeaky the Squirrel sneak out from under Captain Ahoy's pirate hat and hide behind a palm tree.

"Haha, I am the best pirate in the whole wide world," shouted Captain Milk Thirsty Ahoy.

He continued to dig under the giant rainbow castle until his spade went CLUNK. He had hit something. He looked down and saw a huge wooden treasure box. It was covered with golden and silver chains and had a big sign that read "KEEP OUT! PIRATE KING PROPERTY." Before Captain Milk Thirsty Ahoy had time to open the box, he felt something cold spraying into his eyes. He began to feel very sleepy. His eyes began to close, and he collapsed onto the sand with a big bump.

"Hooray!" shouted Squeaky the Squirrel. "My magic reversal potion worked! Now to wake up the P2C pirate crew!"

With some help from a friendly kangaroo, he quickly brewed some more magic reversal potion. They put in some crushed-up shark bones and some glittery pebbles. Squeaky the Squirrel then began to spray it all over the sleeping pirates. They soon began to stretch and yawn and wake up. They all quickly gathered around the wooden treasure box, and Captain Ahoy ordered them back to the ship. They climbed aboard their ship, set the sails, raised the anchor and set off back to Bruntsfield Bay with the special treasure. Once they got there, they gave the treasure to Pirate King Grrrhooley.

P1A

3
BRUNTSFIELD PIRATE SCHOOL
P1A

P1A had just arrived back from their morning break time and were sitting on the carpet drinking pirate milk, practising their pirate phonics by repeating 'arrrrrghhh!' when Pirate King Grrrhooley jumped into the classroom. He told the class some very funny pirate jokes then gave P1A an important task to do.

"Arrrrrrghhhh, ahoy maties," he said. "I have a mission for you! There is treasure in Paris. I hear it is at the very top of the Eiffel Tower. Go get it and bring it back to the school. I've given a map to your captain to find your way."

P1A ran down to Bruntsfield Bay where their ship was anchored. The ship was bigger than the school and stood out amongst the rest for many reasons, and not just for its size! The name of the ship, *Chicken Nugget*, always made people laugh. *Chicken Nugget* was built with left over school lunches. The crew had worked very hard to piece it together and make it ocean-ready. It was made completely out of chicken nuggets which was P1A's favourite pirate food. Obviously!

On arrival, Captain McBanana inspected the outside of the ship for any leaks and added a few more chicken nuggets for repair. She then climbed aboard before the rest of the crew to check that her boat was safe after a few weeks of being empty. Captain McBanana carried over her shoulder a bag full of her own favourite food for their journey—she couldn't spend seven months at sea without bananas.

She gave the go ahead and the rest of the crew started to board. At the front of the line was the captain's pet lion, Candyfloss. Despite being five years old, Candyfloss looked much younger because he was so small. Shortly behind was Achey Fort, the ship's first mate. Achey Fort was wearing a stripy skirt and was smiling even though she was always worrying that she might be the worst swimmer in the crew! She spent a lot of time eating her favourite food pizza with mushrooms, olives and pineapple but never shared! Something she hated the most was candy. She thought sugar was disgusting. No one really knew why, but the crew thought it was probably to do with Captain McBanana making her spend lots of her time flossing the teeth of Candyfloss the lion with floss—well, actually, candyfloss.

Shortly after Achey Fort came Swordface. He was best known for the problems he had because of how he held his sword.... in his mouth. The most important thing to know about Swordface was how often that sword in his mouth got in the way. Every time he relaxed on the deck reading a book, the book quickly got sliced up by the sword. Just as well there wasn't much time for relaxing on *Chicken Nugget*!

The rest of the PiA pirates climbed aboard and off they went. Pirate Lois took charge of directions and insisted that it wasn't a good idea to go directly to Paris by the North Sea and instead "we must sail the seven seas (well, most of them) to avoid any danger."

Setting sail, the journey began long and cold through the Arctic Ocean. The crew thought it was cool to see walruses sliding across the ice and others relaxing. They also saw penguins diving into the water.

Next, it was a hard and choppy sail through the Pacific Ocean where they spotted sharks chasing their prey and jellyfish chasing clown fish. The whole crew agreed that the Pacific Ocean was the most fascinating journey, as they also saw dolphins and orcas jumping out the water.

As they were travelling south in the North Pacific, Lois thought they may as well take in the sights of the South China Sea passing Japan, China and Malaysia. Some of the crew members had hoped to stop in China to visit family members and show their crewmates their family culture, but they all agreed that they could come back another time!

The crew was well into the Indian Ocean when they saw a really long creature that looked like a mermaid and was almost the same size as the ship. For a moment they thought this creature was beginning to attack, so they all got into their ready positions before the captain yelled "Hold fire!" It turned out the creature was not intimidated by the boat but fascinated and had come to check it out.

Once they tackled the Indian Ocean, the pirates continued round the bottom of Africa and into the Atlantic. They were on for a rough journey as the sea kept almost tipping them over. Lots of the crew had to take days off sailing because they were so seasick. Finally, they made it to the English Channel in one piece.

Even though she had worked really hard navigating the world, Pirate Lois still had work to do to find the best route into Paris. Just when the *Chicken Nugget* crew thought they were in safe waters, some crewmates started to notice the boat was not floating correctly...

The boat started to wobble from side to side, and the crew started to notice crumbs in the sea. These crumbs looked suspiciously like the same chicken nugget crumbs left on the dining hall floor! Suddenly, Pirate Noah noticed a large black sea horse rising from under the water. "Look out!" he shouted. Everyone looked off the boat to see Monsterman riding the seahorse having a nibble on some of their essential chicken nuggets! Those on the lower deck started to notice water at their feet and were working quickly to repair the leaks and throw the water overboard. Meanwhile, Swordface jumped into action. He picked up his sword, put it in his mouth and started running towards the edge of the ship. Just when the crew thought he was about to jump overboard into danger, he grabbed a hanging rope with his two available hands and swung himself out above Monsterman and the seahorse.

Impressed with this move, the crew all went running to see what would happen over the edge of the ship. As they all got to the end of boat, Swordface and the rope were falling in the direction of the sea!

"You never learn!!" shouted Captain McBanana, who had realised that the sword that he so proudly held in his mouth had once again caught him in a spot of bother by cutting the rope he was holding on to.

He landed with a plop in the cold sea, and Monsterman was quickly approaching. Swordface was a strong swimmer but was struggling to keep afloat in the rough sea.

Suddenly there was another splash from the other side of the boat. Reappearing at the surface was Candyfloss alongside Achey Fort, who was clinging on with a piece of candy floss still attached between Candyfloss' teeth! Achey Fort was obviously in the middle of her daily chore when the lion leapt into the water to save his crewmate, and she was not happy about it. Achey Fort grabbed hold of Candyfloss' neck and closed her eyes—she really hated swimming.

Candyfloss paddled to Swordface at the speed of a shark and lifted him out of the water.

At that point, Achey Fort realised it was down to her to

defend the ship. "Behind you!" shouted a crewmember. Achey Fort looked round to see Monsterman coming right for them. She jumped up on top of Candyfloss' back and grabbed the sword from Swordface's mouth to prepare herself. She held the sword with one hand and the candy floss with the other to keep her balance and stay out of the water. She knew she only had one chance at success and got into the ready position with the sword above her shoulder.

As Monsterman and the seahorse got closer, Achey Fort swung with all her force. It went silent. She stood still and waited. The crew watching on realised she had her eyes closed. Everyone looked to Monsterman who had fallen from the back of the black seahorse. Achey Fort opened her eyes to see that she had knocked him from his ride and a big smile appeared across her face.

"I surrender!" shouted Monsterman to Captain McBanana.

After deciding what to do with Monsterman, the crew lowered a wooden box into the sea that Captain McBanana had put some of her bananas in and suggested Monsterman climb in. Rather than leaving him stranded and floating on his own, the crew of PiA decided to let him float ashore on his own with a bit of food. That way he might have time to think about what he had done.

Climbing aboard to a round of applause from the crew, Achey Fort was beaming with pride! It didn't matter that she couldn't swim, she used resilience and other skills to put her mind to the task at hand.

Swordface looked sad and upset. He had, again, made a silly mistake with his sword.

"Don't worry," said Captain McBanana, holding his shoulder, "we can spend the next few days showing you different ways to hold and use your sword. For now, just keep it in the sheath." The rest of the crew then crowded around him giving, him cuddles to make him feel better.

When the crew arrived in Paris, they set anchor right in the centre where they could see the Eiffel Tower above the buildings! Everyone was very excited to get off the boat, and before all thirty of them started to make a dash for the treasure, they realised there was no detail on the map for when they were in Paris, so they stopped in a café for directions. Captain McBanana asked a man drinking his morning coffee what direction the Eiffel Tower was.

"You all seem in a hurry. Why are you looking for Eiffel Tower so early in the morning?" said the man in crooked voice.

Captain McBanana had a strange feeling about this man, but before she could warn the crew, Swordface had blurted out that there was treasure at the top of the Eiffel Tower.

"Aha, you'll regret telling Stinky Socks that!" the man said as he started to throw stinky socks at Captain McBanana.

Captain McBanana fainted at the smell and was unable to lead the crew the rest of the way. Leaving Captain McBanana behind, the crew split up. Achey Fort and Swordface found access to a helicopter and very quickly got to the top of the Eiffel Tower, but Stinky Socks had already beaten them to the destination. Before they had time to defend themselves, Stinky Socks quickly started throwing stinky socks at the helicopter. One particularly big smelly sock landed straight in the face of Achey Fort, who instantly fell flat on her back, fainting at the smell of the sock.

Now it was down to Swordface on his own!

Grabbing what he could out of Achey Fort's bag to throw, he saw lots of left over candyfloss. He started to notice Stinky Socks becoming weaker and weaker the more he threw. Once Swordface ran out of candyfloss, he noticed Stinky Sock was so weak he had stopped throwing socks.

Swordface took the opportunity to jump from the helicopter to the top of the Eiffel Tower. He landed on both feet with his sword still safely in its sheath. Stinky Socks was laying on the floor, still too weak to protect the treasure for himself. Working quickly and resisting the urge to put his sword in his mouth, Swordface picked up the treasure and was just about to jump back to the helicopter when Stinky Socks started to show signs of energy returning. Swordface threw the treasure on to the hovering helicopter and pulled out his sword from his sheath. Captain McBanana had been giving him lessons to use a sword in both hands. Using his right hand he pointed the sword towards Stinky Socks angrily which was enough to warn him not to throw anymore socks. Swordface didn't need to know that Stinky Socks had run out of socks to throw anyway!

Swordface jumped onto the helicopter, which scooped him up. It flew off with the treasure back to the boat. Once they arrived back on the boat, Achey Fort and Captain McBanana had recovered from the stinky socks, and the rest of the crew were waiting for them. The treasure chest dropped down with a thud on to the deck. "We better get this back to Pirate King Grrrhooley to find out what is in here!"

Off the *Chicken Nugget* sailed back across the North Sea to Edinburgh where the captain delivered the precious cargo to Pirate King Grrrhooley.

P4/5

4

CRAZY CANADIAN COASTER

P4/5

The sun was rising over the pirate stronghold, Bruntsfield Bay. Captain Callypso and her P4/5 crew were boarding their ship the *Sea Skull*. They had been sent by Pirate King Grrrhooley to get one of the twenty-one treasures of the world. But would they manage to get through some fiendish obstacles in their way?

The *Sea Skull* was brown and had metal rims with gold buttons. The ship was a sloop and was good at sinking ships. However, manoeuvrability was one of its weaknesses.

Crate after crate after crate went into the hold of the ship. They were full of supplies needed for the journey. In went five barrels of cola, followed by ten more crates with bottles of water, then fifty packs of Oreos and seventy peanut butter sandwiches with jam on top and barrels with granola bars, Irn Bru and pancakes.

Billy Bones was meant to be supervising the packing but had munched all the amazingly delicious waffles for the journey. Captain Callypso had to take over the supervising of the packing so there would be no more munching!

Billy Bones was now fitting his shiny new metal arm while

Lunar Cherry the dragon was secretly devouring the cherry cupcakes packed for the journey. In the meantime, Shakira was doing as she was told by putting down the hay bedding for the crew and Lunar Cherry's neon cat bed.

They had to repair everyone's weapons and check them in case they encountered danger on the way. They also had to check the mega cork cannon at the bow of the ship. The cannon could fire corks in any direction at any attacker. It had a cork on a string that pulled back because you could never know what might happen along the way. In went the ammunition for it—four crates of cork.

When they finally finished loading supplies, weapons and of course themselves, the crew was ready to unfurl the sails. Who knew if they would come back alive, or indeed with the treasure?

The *Sea Skull* set off from Edinburgh into the murky sea. The next day, the *Sea Skull* arrived at John o' Groats and then passed Orkney. After hours of travelling, they finally got away from Scotland and into the vast open ocean. They entered the North Atlantic Ocean and headed southwest of the Labrador Sea.

The crew was ready to turn south towards the Gulf of St Lawrence while Billy Bones was opening Oreo wrappers at the rim of the *Sea Skull*. Unfortunately, he accidentally cut himself, and some blood dripped into the water, spreading out like a red cloud. Seconds later, an ominous grey shape appeared and broke the surface of the water. It was shooting towards him at an insane speed, causing the boat to rock violently as the waves crashed against the boat really loudly.

Lunar Cherry, who was down below in her cabin, sensed something wrong and woke Captain Callypso from her deep sleep. Captain Callypso asked her what was wrong. Lunar Cherry the dragon replied in a squeaky breathless voice, "Shark ahead!"

Suddenly there was a net of dark grey clouds covering the sky which reflected the mood of the now-terrified crew. Billy Bones ran ahead and said, "That's not a normal shark. IT'S A MEGALODON!"

The megalodon was a monumental dark grey monster, sixty-nine feet long with 276 humungous serrated teeth and glowing red eyes full of hatred. It normally lived in the depths of the ocean.

It disappeared under the water, then suddenly jumped out of the ocean at the other side of the ship with jaws open, ready to chomp up the *Sea Skull*. The megalodon's huge jaw snapped at the hull of the *Sea Skull,* baring its teeth and tearing off the rusty metal railing running along the side of the ship. The pirates were paralysed with fear to the point that Billy Bones wet his pants.

The megalodon slammed its tail into the ship, sending the ship spinning out of control and bringing the pirates back to their senses. Then the pirates fought back.

Billy Bones, who had recovered from his shock, ran down to the mega cork cannon. He fired a cork which hit the megalodon on the snout. But before Billy Bones could pull it back, it had already disappeared into the stomach of the megalodon. Billy Bones reloaded a cork into the cannon and fired it again.

Now the battle really escalated. The mega cork cannon was fired again and again, which made the megalodon more and more angry and aggressive. Pistols were fired and swords slashed. The battle was epic! The pirates had to face it, this could easily be their last day on Earth... Then suddenly Billy Bones had the brightest idea in human history! "Everyone, get the cabbage supplies," he yelled, "and hand them all to me." One by one the crew handed the cabbage supplies to him, and he stuffed them in Lunar Cherry's mouth. Suddenly, just in time as the megalodon tried to bite the ship to pieces, Lunar Cherry did the biggest fart in the history of the world. She outgassed the megalodon, and while it was disorientated, she did another few farts which propelled the ship forward speedily into the distance. The crew was safe for another day.

After defeating the megalodon, they entered the Gulf of St Lawrence. Captain Callypso got more and more stressed about the immigration officer, Captain Grumpy Pants, who had very strict immigration rules. Shakira soon noticed that Captain Callypso was getting more pale by the minute, so she decided to ask her if everything was alright.

Captain Callypso decided to share her fears about Captain Grumpy Pants, and Shakira soon realised why she was so worried and told the rest of the crew. As they rowed along the winding river, they pulled down the flag to cover their identity. They realised they had to put on disguises, so they took costumes from the barracks. Shakira put on an itchy wig and a scruffy shawl. Billy Bones pulled out an inflatable dinosaur suit because there was a pink tutu that he did not like. Captain Callypso raced to get changed into a black cloak and jeans.

As they entered the Canadian border, they saw Canadian flags, which caused Captain Callypso to pause for a second to think. "I should have guessed!" she exclaimed. "Captain Grumpy Pants, the leader of Canada's immigration office is going to try to stop us from entering!" Captain Grumpy Pants was the strictest, most horrible immigration officer in the world. He had a big green beard and a parrot which he taught to say rude words.

Finally, they reached Lake Ontario, but Captain Grumpy Pants spotted them straight away. As they jumped off the *Sea Skull,* he fired a net, which Lunar Cherry caught in mid-air and threw back at him. This turned Grumpy Pants into Furious Pants, so he sent out his evil golden robot army!

Soon Shakira and Billy Bones noticed a huge flaw in the robots: They were powered by maple syrup. This meant if they got enough bugs into their system, they would slowly break down. But there was one major problem in this plan: Shakira HATED bugs! However, Shakira knew that Captain Callypso and the crew were counting on her, so she faced her fears and threw the bugs into the robots system. Billy Bones punched one but got covered in maple syrup and got stuck in the gooey mixture. Shakira helped Billy Bones out of the maple syrup. When Billy Bones was free, they fought the golden robots with all their might.

Captain Callypso ordered Billy Bones and Shakira to get as many bugs as they could. Billy Bones soon had a huge collection of bugs in his hands and looked quite grossed out. He threw all the bugs at the attacking robots, and, one by one, they went berserk and collapsed to the deck and were shut down for good.

The bugs had eaten the sweet maple syrup fuelling the robots and had killed them! The crew were saved for now...

They passed Quebec and after that Montreal, and then the crew were ready to enter Lake Ontario. When they did, they slowed the ship until it got to the narrowest part of the river and docked on the elegant wooden pier.

Finally the P4/5 crew were ready to get off the ship. It was going to be a long walk, so they took the bus to the stop nearest to the theme park. Eventually the pirates reached Canada's Wonderland in Ontario where Captain Callypso drew a map of the Amusement Park out of her pocket. The crew was astonished by how terrifying the rides looked, and Lunar Cherry had a face that suggested that she was not going on any of them. On the way to the Leviathan, they saw Swing of the Century, Swan Lake and Taxi Run. Leviathan was the tallest and fastest rollercoaster in Canada's Wonderland in Vaughan, Ontario. At 1,672 metres long and 93.3 metres high, it towered over the rest of the roller coasters and activities in the park.

Billy, Shakira and Lunar Cherry joined the line for the roller coaster. When it was finally their turn, they got on and prepared to do what they had been sent there to do. Billy Bones, Shakira and Lunar Cherry got on board Leviathan because it was their mission to take the treasure box suspended on the roller coaster rail back to Pirate King Grrrhooley. It was suspended on the top of a bump, so Billy and Shakira had to jump from the bottom of the bump, grab the treasure and land back in their rollercoaster carriage.

When they got to the highest point (after lot of big dips and loop-the-loops) Billy spied the treasure box on the underside of a bump and took his seat belt off. Suddenly he jumped without warning and dislodged the treasure box from its place. Shakira grabbed him by his feet and dragged him back in the carriage. He had retrieved the treasure box, which was a rose gold clam that they were not able to open because it was too tightly sealed.

"I have it!" he whispered. "I have the treasure." He showed Shakira the box and then quickly hugged it tight to himself as the roller coaster stopped. As they got off, Captain Calypso and the crew congratulated them for getting the treasure.

Then they spotted their ship and hopped over the parking thingymajiggy or what they thought was a parking barrier. Captain Callypso realised the ship was a ride but it was fun. Billy Bones spotted another ship ride. Shakira and Captain Callypso said, "That is another ride, you doughnut. The *Sea Skull* is in the other direction." After a hot dog and a drink, the crew went to the bus stop to get the bus to the docks where the ship was. The treasure was theirs and they were ready to go home. But before they boarded the ship, they stopped off at Tim Hortons for five barrels of maple syrup.

The crew were setting off from the docks as they notice that someone was on the roof of the bridge. Shakira looked up and saw Captain Grumpy Pants with his parrot. Once he noticed that the crew knew he was there, he shot his net at the pirates, but the skilled Lunar Cherry caught it and then shot out a fart that she had been saving. And while the crew put on gas masks, Captain Grumpy Pants got completely knocked out.

Billy Bones dragged the unconscious Captain Grumpy Pants and stuffed him into the mega cork cannon. He fired the cannon, and Captain Grumpy Pants flew through the air into the window of his office on the dock.

They had the bright idea of taking a slightly different route home in case the megalodon still lingered where they'd last seen it. As they sailed along the edge of the Labrador Sea, a massive gust of wind picked them up and blew them right across the Atlantic Ocean. The crew sailed all the way to Edinburgh through calm seas. When they got to Bruntsfield, they handed the pirate treasure over to Pirate King Grrrhooley and wondered what would happen next...

P2B

5

THE ATTACK OF SQUIRTY AND THE HOBBITS

P2B

It was an icy cold morning at Leith Docks in Edinburgh. Thick fog surrounded the harbour. Bright flashes of lightning shot through the sky. A young girl had stopped to tie her shoelaces at the docks. As she stood up and looked out to the water, she noticed a large shadow coming towards her through the fog. At first she thought it was just a rain cloud, but it got bigger and bigger. Then she thought it might be the Loch Ness Monster. A flash of lightning suddenly hit the shadow, and she realised that, in fact, it was a pirate ship!

The ship slowly came closer into the docks. The young girl noticed that there was writing along the side of the ship that said, "Bruntsfield Invaders". The girl had heard of these pirates before and knew better than to wait around.

Standing on the deck of the ship was Captain Doiiig, Captain Farty and Captain Poppy. They were some of the scariest pirates around. No one liked to mess with them.

Captain Doiiig looked a little like Cruella de Vil. Half of her hair was black, the other half was white. On the top of her head she wore a hat with a skull and crossbones. On her shoulder sat her pet called Fire Fang. Captain Doiiig had found Fire Fang during a treasure hunt on an isolated island in the middle of the Mediterranean Sea. Fire Fang had the body of a Komodo dragon, the pointy nose of a rat and the tail of a monkey. And let's not forget two pointed fangs that could shoot fireballs at the speed of light!

Captain Farty was tall and thin. He had green hair and a green curly moustache which often contained crumbs of the last meal he had eaten. He wore a dirty green vest covered in stains, and he smelled like a rubbish dump.

Captain Poppy had hair as red as fire. She wore a poppy tiara crown and a black dress covered in poppies. She had a bright blue parrot called Bongo Heid and she wouldn't go anywhere without him.

As the ship pulled into the shore, the three captains dropped the anchor and boarded the docks. Standing at the edge of the docks was Pirate King Grrrhooley. As soon as the captains noticed him, they bowed in his honour.

He announced that he needed the three captains' help in locating some hidden treasure. The captains smiled and laughed; finding hidden treasure was easy for them. Pirate King Grrrhooley then announced that Captain Green Beard was also trying to find the treasure and may have set some traps for them along the way.

Captain Farty let out a silent but violent fart. He always farted when he was nervous.

Captain Grrrhooley handed the captains a treasure map, and at the top of the map it said "New Zealand" in huge letters.

"That's halfway around the world!" shouted Captain Poppy.

"You're right," said Captain Grrrhooley. "So you better get a move on." And so the three captains set off on their biggest adventure yet.

After almost four months at sea, the captains were exhausted from their travels. The sea was angry and rough, but they only had about one week of travel left before they reached

New Zealand. The three captains were taking a well-deserved nap on the deck of the ship when they were rudely awakened by a large bang against the side of the ship. They peered over into the water, but they couldn't see anything.

"Maybe we just hit a rock," exclaimed Captain Doiiig. They laid back down. Just as they closed their eyes, there was another loud bang at the side of the ship. This time it was so hard that Fire Fang was flung across to the opposite side of the ship.

Suddenly a huge monster appeared in the ocean. It was a kraken.

This was no normal kraken. This was one of the deadliest sea monsters around—this was Squirty. It was colossal in size and had huge bright green dragon wings and piercing red eyes. Its flashing purple tentacle latched onto the side of the ship and ripped off a large chunk of wood.

Squirty let out an enormous roar similar to the roar of a dinosaur. It was so loud that it knocked Captain Doiiig out cold. Luckily Captain Poppy and Captain Farty's ears were covered by their hats. Unfortunately, Captain Doiiig's hat had been knocked off by the rocking of the ship.

Captain Poppy was furious. She called on Bongo Heid for help. Bongo Heid made a loud squawk and suddenly hundreds of other parrots surrounded the ship. They dived into the ocean and resurfaced with treasure of their own. In their beaks they held seaweed, clams and shells.

"Attack!" screamed Captain Poppy.

The parrots threw the items at Squirty with force. Squirty tried to shield himself with his tentacles and let go of the ship. The parrots kept firing things at him until he slid back under the ocean's surface.

"Do you think he's gone?" asked Captain Farty. Just as the words left his mouth, Squirty flew up from the ocean. His dragon wings were spread out in the sky, and every time he flapped his wings, fire shot out of them. One of the fire balls hit the ship.

Captain Farty was terrified of fire and let out another nervous fart. The smell was so bad that when Captain Poppy smelled it she passed out.

Captain Farty was the only one left standing. This made him even more nervous, and the farts just wouldn't stop. Squirty kept shooting fire at the ship and Captain Farty kept trying to hide while farting. The gases coming out of his bottom were so strong that when he let out a final huge fart it reacted with the fire and caused a humongous explosion.

The explosion hit Squirty, and he fell from the sky and crashed into the ocean. Captain Farty jumped with joy and celebrated. He ran over to Captain Doiiig and Captain Poppy to wake them up. They were so delighted and surprised that he had defeated Squirty by himself.

Just as they were about to take sail again, a huge tentacle swept up from the ocean and onto the ship. It grabbed Fire Fang and Captain Doiiig, pulling them into the ocean. The other captains tried to save them, but it was too late. Squirty had taken them.

Captain Poppy and Captain Farty had to continue their journey a captain down. They finally arrived at New Zealand and anchored the ship. They looked at their treasure map and headed into the forest. Soon after, they noticed a treasure chest. It wasn't where it was supposed to be on the map.

"It could be a trap left by Green Beard," cried Captain Poppy.

"Don't be so silly, he's not clever enough to leave traps," replied Captain Farty. Captain Farty ran towards the treasure chest, and Captain Poppy ran after him to stop him. As soon as they got close, they tripped on a rope, and an anvil fell from a tree.

"That nearly hit me," said Captain Farty.

"I told you it was a trap," moaned Captain Poppy.

They kept walking and suddenly were swept up in a large net. Flaming arrows started shooting at them from the trees. The captains had to swing the net from side to side to avoid getting hit. Unfortunately, one of the arrows brushed against the rope and set the net on fire. But Captain Poppy remembered that she had a cutlass in her belt and cut the rope, setting them free.

They continued their adventure into the forest.

Captain Poppy and Captain Farty kept following the map. They were getting close to the real treasure when they heard chattering. It was coming from behind a large bush. They poked their heads through the bush and saw a large group of hobbits sitting in a circle. In the middle of the circle was the treasure chest. The captains had no idea how they were going to be able to get past all these hobbits.

Captain Farty started to get nervous again, and his belly began to rumble. Captain Poppy was worried he was going to do a fart so smelly that she would pass out again.

His face went red. He couldn't help it. He was going to let out another nervous fart. He clenched his bum cheeks tight, but then a small fart escaped from his bottom. It made a loud squeak.

The hobbits turned to face the bush where the captains were hiding. He had an idea. "Hold your breath," he said to Captain Poppy. As she did, Captain Farty began to let out loads of farts. But the farts didn't sound like normal farts. They sounded almost musical, similar to the noise of a chanter. He sprinted off into the woods, letting out his squeaky farts as he ran.

The hobbits loved music, and this was the best tune they had heard all year. They chased after the music, dancing and ready to party.

Captain Poppy was delighted; the treasure had been left

alone! She grabbed it and ran as fast as she could back to the beach. As she arrived, she saw Captain Farty running towards her.

"Get back on the ship!" he shouted. Captain Poppy spotted lots of hobbits chasing after him. The hobbits must have realised they had been tricked and were now running to get their treasure back.

They started throwing stones at the captains and waved swords and axes. Although they were small, they were fierce, and there was no way the captains could take them all on.

Just as they were about to give back the treasure, Squirty shot up from the ocean. On his back were Captain Doiiig and Fire Fang! When they had been pulled into the water, they had thought they were goners. Squirty had such a tight grip of them. However, they managed to escape danger by tickling Squirty and making him their friend. Squirty loved tickles.

Fire Fang shot balls of fire at the hobbits, and Squirty sprayed his ink onto the beach. The hobbits all started to slide around like Bambi on ice. The hobbits that didn't fall over were scared off by the fire and ran back into the woods.

The captains celebrated their victory and thanked Squirty for his help. They finally boarded back onto their ship and set sail to bring the treasure chest back to Pirate King Grrrhooley.

When they arrived back at the docks, they gave Pirate King Grrrhooley the treasure, wondering what was inside the box.

P6A

Ruki

6

JOURNEY TO DAHAB

P6A

The P6A pirates were enjoying some coconut water as they were sitting at Pirate Bay's pub. A fiddler played a cheery tune on a stool in the corner, and a gentle breeze blew through the open windows. Suddenly, the door burst open as Pirate King Grrrhooley entered excitedly with a brown sheet of paper in his hand! Pirate King Grrrhooley strutted over with a big grin on his face.

"As my most independent and resilient pirates, I need you to travel across the sea towards the ancient land of Egypt," he exclaimed with a devilish glint in his eyes.

He spread out a world map on the wooden table in front of First Mate Belinda, First Mate Jack and Captain Lilly and pointed to a thin blue line running through the country. Captain Lilly Patrick Brown squinted at the page, her eyes finding it difficult to see in the dimly lit room.

"Travel along the Suez Canal until you reach the city of Dahab. In this city, hidden in the most difficult to reach place, lies some treasure." He paused. "It is said to be the most magnificent treasure that has ever existed," whispered Pirate King Grrrhooley.

Jack, who hated seeing anyone sad or disappointed, jumped up with glee.

"Of course we'll do it!" he shouted. He was already thinking about the kind of pizza toppings that would be eaten in Egypt.

"But nobody has been successful in completing this daring and intimidating quest, so I don't know the exact dangers that await you," Grrrhooley warned. The table was quiet.

"Capisce?" he asked.

"Capisce!" yelled the P6A pirates. The rest of the crew had wandered over to the table and were now huddled around, tingling with excitement.

Grrrhooley handed Captain Lilly a big treasure map that was ripped and tattered with age and, without saying anything else, walked out. The door slammed behind him.

The P6A pirates left the pub and hurried back to their ship, *Hasirugomi,* which was anchored by the jetty. It was a beautiful ship and all of the pirates loved calling it their home. It was made out of a dark brown wood with each of the pirates names etched into the side. Unlike most other pirate ships, *Hasirugomi*'s sails were brightly coloured with artworks by the pirates that lived aboard.

They knew what needed to be done without being told, so they all set to work hoisting the sails and lifting the anchor ready to leave Pirate Bay.

As they sailed over the restless sea, waves lapped at the ships stern. Suddenly, First Mate Belinda heard and felt a disturbing *thud, thud, thud.* She looked over the side of the ship and saw that it was not the water that was rippling; it was a school of vicious sword fish tossing all their might into the ship and creating punctures in the wood!

The ship began filling up with water, but Captain Lilly Patrick Brown had an idea and tried to scare the sword fish away by grabbing a rope and jumping off the side of the boat.

She kicked and swung her free arms and legs in karate moves, but unfortunately it didn't work.

Fortunately, Belinda had a better idea. She cut off clumps of her thick curly hair with a pair of rusty scissors and made sponges to plug the holes and stop the ship from sinking. The crew held their breath while they waited to see if it would work.

Thankfully, it did. Belinda had saved the day.

From then on, the P6A pirates a peaceful journey to Dahab. Tiny, the P6A mascot, lay in the sun on the deck. Tiny looked like a fox, although he had nine bright purple, scaly tails instead of one and a chest with long grey fur. His ears were also longer than a fox's and his eyes were more tear-shaped. As he lay in the sun, his nine tails slithered like snakes around his body and his fur danced in the wind.

The crew could feel the floorboards creaking beneath their feet. Lilly Patrick Brown stood at the helm steering the ship and keeping a watchful eye of her crew. Jack and Belinda were enjoying watching the calm, blue ocean and the bright, warm sun. They knew how quickly these conditions could change. Just like in Scotland, they knew they needed to appreciate it while it lasted.

Clearly exhausted and dehydrated after the long and stressful journey they'd already had, the crew walked down the gangway and stepped onto the burning sand of Dahab.

"Oweee!" the crew cried as they jumped from foot to foot in the burning sand.

Tiny, whose tough paw pads were able to take the heat, smirked at his friends jumping around like frogs.

They certainly did not think of this when they considered the treacherous conditions of Egypt. As they set off into the desert, their eyes felt like they had been cut by razor blades as the sand got into their eyes and blocked their view. They looked up to see a sandstorm rolling towards them. The crew began to panic. The sand whipped all of them and stung their skin. The pirates couldn't move. Out of the corner of a very squinted eye, Belinda could see a small narrow building in the distance. She could see that the sand was not as strong and vicious there.

"Hey you guys, look!" she bellowed. "There's a house in the distance! The sand looks more gentle there!"

"Oh come on, Belinda, you must be out of this world. There ain't no house here. It's just an illusion," said Jack, struggling to talk with all the sand in his mouth.

"But I really see it!" replied Belinda, sounding hoarse. Her voice cracked with the force of the biting sand.

"Well it's worth a try, aye? Let's go," said Lilly, getting desperate.

When they arrived they saw that the building was much less welcoming than it looked in the distance. The windows were cracked and they could not see any lights on inside. There was a sign which was hanging by one measly chain. It read: QUICKSAND CASINO.

"You brought us to a casino? Great job, Belinda," said Jack sarcastically. Jack was usually very nice, but he hadn't eaten pizza in a while which could make him rather unpleasant.

"Be quiet," said Lilly. "A casino is a better place to stay than none."

"It looks too shabby to be a real casino," commented Jack as they pushed open the doors and stepped inside.

The casino was dark and tired looking. The slot machines seemed to be fifty years old and mismatched chairs sat in front of old plastic card tables. Most of these seemed to be broken. There were ten sinister looking pirates dotted around the room, who stared at the P6A crew as they entered.

"These people are gambling!" said Lilly, shocked.

The crew found a few big tables nearby, ordered some drinks and sat down to talk.

"Have any of you seen Tiny?" asked Jack, looking around for their friend.

"Why no, nowhere," said Belinda carelessly, shrugging her shoulders. She took her mug of rum and had a nice long sip.

"Well, he was on the ship with us. He can't have just disappeared," replied Jack, looking worried.

Without warning, a revolting looking a man appeared by their table. He was smeared with dirt and dust all over. His eye patch was as big as a normal human hand, and his disgusting nose, which was a peculiar shape, was maybe the size of his two ginormous feet put together. He looked like a giant from those Irish folk tales.

"Ahem, and who might you be, brother?" asked Lilly, trying to be brave but trembling with fear.

" Me name's Big Nose Bucklebutt, and I'll ask the questions here, missy," the giant replied.

"Yes Big Butt, I-I mean Big Nose, sir," replied Lilly.

"Hmm, come, let's play a poker game," said Big Nose, staring at her.

"Ok," said Lily, her fear easing slightly. She was good at poker.

They played a great match; both Lilly and Big Nose had very lucky cards, but in the end, Lilly won! There were shouts of joy and encouragement from the other P6A pirates. Big Nose, however, was furious. He turned a purple reddish colour and grabbed Lilly with his great hands, unable to control his anger. He stormed off with Lilly under one of his arms. The crew stood too shocked and frightened to move as Big Nose carried Lilly through a door at the back of the room.

"Hey, wait a minute, that's one of Tiny's tails in his big nose!" exclaimed Jack.

Jack was right. Twitching from one of Big Nose's enormous nostrils like a trapped worm was a shiny purple tail that the crew knew very well.

Big Nose carried Lilly into a small room that was bare apart from a single slot machine in the corner. It looked even older than the rest of them. Big Nose yanked open the machine with his big hand and shoved Lilly into a tiny and very dark corner in the back of the huge machine. He took a padlock from his jacket pocket and, with a click, locked Lilly inside.

She felt helpless as she knew her crew wouldn't be able to hear her cries for help.

But Jack and Belinda were, as usual, looking out for Lilly and had kept a close eye on Big Nose when he took her away. They knew they couldn't go after her while Big Nose was with her, so they sat down, ordered some pizza from the dirty casino kitchen and waited.

When Big Nose appeared from the room where he took Lilly, Jack and Belinda knew they had to work quickly. They formed a plan with the rest of the crew and snuck into the room. The crew announced that there would be an arm wrestling match in the pub and the winner would win a cask of coconut water. Everyone in the casino seemed keen, even Big Nose. The crew hoped this would be a good distraction.

Inside the small room, Jack and Belinda rushed over to the slot machine, realising Lilly couldn't be anywhere else, and helped her out. As the three of them left the room, they signalled to the rest of the crew to follow them in their quest for the legendary treasure.

They searched and searched across the dry hot desert. The map told them that the treasure should be there, but all they could see was a sea of golden sand. First Mate Jack sat down in frustration on a rock.

Suddenly, a giant pyramid rose up majestically from the sand, and Jack slid down it which caused incredible friction on his bottom.

"Let's go in!" cried Belinda, leading the crew inside the pyramid through a stone arch.

The inside was bare. "There's nothing here. We must have

come to the wrong pyramid!" exclaimed Captain Lilly in a disappointed tone.

Suddenly, the ground started to shake and sink.

"Guys, it's quicksand!" shouted Jack as they fell through the floor.

They all landed with a thump on the ground in a big heap. They looked around and saw the walls were stacked with coffins, and they could see the treasure box glittering in the light.

They lunged for it, and suddenly Big Nose appeared from nowhere.

"You aren't going to get your grubby little hands on that treasure, because I'm going to get it instead!" he bellowed, grinning.

Then, out of the blue, there came a groaning sound and a shifting noise. All the coffins opened abruptly, and the mummies inside sat up and started walking towards them, dust falling from their bandaged bodies.

The crew tried to run, but they were too frozen with fear, and they couldn't see because there was dust everywhere! Big Nose Bucklebutt inhaled sharply and did a great big slimy sneeze! All the mummies were coated in Big Nose's mucus! The mummies tried to move but were rooted to the spot.

Tiny, who had been sneezed out of Big Nose's nose, jumped with joy. Big Nose, shocked by the force of his ferocious sneeze, swayed and fell over. He hit his head and lay unconscious.

"Ugh," said Belinda as she saw the horrible mucus covering the room.

"What are we going to do with him?" said Lilly.

"I don't know," said Jack, removing his sword from his belt and slashing it through the air.

"Let's get out of here," Belinda said.

"We have to do away with Big Nose first, otherwise we'll

never be sure we are safe, and he might try to steal the treasure again," said Lilly. The rest of the crew nodded in agreement.

Then Tiny started moving his tails in a peculiar manner. He first waved his tails toward the mummies and then at Big Nose.

"Wow! Good idea, Tiny!" said Jack, ruffling her fur.

"What?" asked Belinda and Lilly, not sure what Tiny was suggesting.

"We'll tie him to the ceiling with the mummies bandages," explained Jack.

The crew thought this was a great plan, so together, with the help of Tiny, they unwrapped a bandage from a mummy and tied Big Nose to the ceiling. Then they triumphantly marched out into the sunshine. Tiny's beautiful tails stuck proudly in the air, and her nose was poised up towards the hot sun.

The pirates of P6A where ecstatic to find out what would be in the chest, which Belinda and Jack were carrying between them.

"What if there's gold or even... DIAMONDS? Or magical stones like sapphires, rubies or emeralds?" exclaimed one of the crew.

The crew were fairly quiet as they walked back. Everyone was deep in thought about the contents of the treasure chest. It was a long walk back to the ship, but when the very familiar outline of the *Hashirugomi* finally came into view bobbing in the sea ahead of them, they were so relieved that they ran the rest of the way. The treasure box was heavy, but Jack and Belinda didn't care.

They climbed aboard and set about doing their jobs: hoisting the sails, raising the anchor and pulling up the gangway.

They glided over the waves with tremendous speed, heading back to Bruntsfield Pirate Bay. They were all so anxious and excited to see what was in the huge wooden box that they were jumping off the walls!

"Calm down, you lot! I am sure that we will find out soon enough," shouted Captain Lilly. Knowing that she was right, the P6A pirates settled down and enjoyed the long journey back. Once they arrived, they gave the box to Pirate King Gr-rrhooley, excited to see what was inside.

P3A

7

THE HUNT IS ON!

P3A

Stomp, stomp, stomp!
Does every pirate king of a pirate school need to be heard before they are seen?

Pirate King Grrrhooley finally appeared and demanded, "Stop your digging!"

The P3A pirate crew paused their digging practice. Kevin "accidentally" (on purpose) threw mud in Pirate King Grrrhooley's face! This wasn't the first time, and it was unlikely to be the last. Pirate King Grrrhooley would get his trusted Admiral Lamond to deal with that one later!

Pirate King Grrrhooley had an important announcement. He told the crewmates about an unspeakable adventure. He told them that the mission was to find the treasure that was buried in the deepest darkest Peru and return it to him unopened.

Captain Hunt and her trusted Parrot Peck Peck were given the mission to lead the P3A pirate crew to deepest darkest Peru. Captain Hunt was the bravest pirate teacher that ever existed in the seven seas. She had an incredible sense of smell that could sniff out villains from several miles away. She was one fierce leader and gave Pirate King Grrrhooley and his admirals a run for their money! Some would say she was the most heroic of all. Her laser sharp dark eyes could reflect light faster than anything else. Her deadly light hair could whip someone out in seconds.

Flying in the gorgeous blue sky was the amazing Peck Peck, Captain Hunt's pet parrot. Peck Peck sat on Captain Hunt's shoulder and pecked to get her attention while the Captain was instructing her loyal crew. Peck Peck was always pecking for the Captain's attention! Peck Peck would peck peck!

Ignoring Peck Peck's pecks, Captain Hunt explained that the treasure was believed to be hidden in the Peruvian jungle stuck in the Tree of Rhythm.

Speeding into the P3A pirate dock with a loud screeching brake arrived the *Messi Siu*. Boarding the most up-to-date pirate ship was Captain Hunt and her loyal crew of thirty. There were thirty rooms and thirty toilets on board the gigantic ship. The ship was known for taking out every villain in its path.

As it arrived, the ship was crowded by the rocks, but this was no problem for the *Messi Siu*. It chomped up the rocks as it docked.

As Captain Hunt and her crew boarded the *Messi Sui*, Peck Peck flew off her shoulder and sat on a perch.

Captain Hunt could only rely on one sailor, and that was Pirate Petersen. Pirate Petersen was the slickest sailor of the seven seas. Pirate Petersen had blue hair and was very adventurous. She was very kind and helpful. At night Pirate Petersen made the beds for the crew. Her lovely eyes sparkled in the sunshine and her blue hair glistened in the moonlight.

Pirate Petersen started the engine. *Vrrooooom!* The ship was pushed into action. The purring sound vibrated through the ship and the waves began to ripple around the bow. The *Messi Sui*'s unspeakable journey launched.

As the *Messi Sui* zoomed through the Atlantic Ocean, the

waves crashed up and over the sides of the ship. A pump cleverly designed by Pirate Petersen cleared the sea water from the deck. The propellers of the ship pushed the water to the sides so it glided through.

While the pirate crew were drying themselves off, something rose from the depths of the Atlantic Ocean. Captain Hunt realised it was a giant megalodon, an extinct prehistoric shark. The megalodon chased the pirate ship. It was larger than a pirate classroom.

Captain Hunt took control of the situation and told her crew to stay at their posts. Harron, a future pirate leader in Captain Hunt's crew, convinced the megalodon to stick his nose out of the water by luring him with some tasty fishy treats. The *Messi Siu* shot a flying football towards its nose. The megalodon hated anything near its nose, so it disappeared into the depths of the Atlantic Ocean and headed towards the South Pacific.

The P3A crew worked hard to support Pirate Petersen as she steered round the icebergs scattered in the Atlantic Ocean. It felt like one became two icebergs and two became four! Nervously the crew clung onto the sides of the ship as it rocked from side to side. Once they dodged the icebergs, the sea opened up and the sun was appearing at the break of dawn. South America was finally in sight.

Peck Peck swooped onto Captain Hunt's shoulder. Captain Hunt said, "Get off, Peck Peck!" and Peck Peck repeated, "Get off, Peck Peck, squawk, squawk!" Captain Hunt repeated the instruction to get off, and Peck Peck mimicked once again!

This could go on and on, Captain Hunt thought. Just as she was about to give up, she realised Peck Peck was trying to warn her of...

Something in the *Messi Siu*'s path. It looked to be red and blue. What could possibly be red and blue in the deepest darkest Peru? Captain Hunt and Peck Peck looked at each other, wondering the exact same thing. Could it really be? Captain

Hunt announced, "Could it be Mr Fart-Maker?" and Peck Peck repeated, "Could it be Mr Fart-Maker, squawk, squawk?!" Captain Hunt sighed, "That's what I said!" and Peck Peck repeated this!

There on a pumice stone was a small bear with a red hat and a blue coat calling out, "I'd like some honey!" It wasn't Mr Fart-Maker, it was Piddington, a well-known bear's cousin! Turns out that the soggy paper Piddington was holding onto was a map. He must know where the treasure is hidden.

Piddington shared that the treasure was actually hidden in the Temple of Doom! Piddington had always wanted to be a pirate with their magnificent swords, eye patches and slick black jackets, so he was more than happy to lead Captain Hunt and the P3A crew of thirty fantabulous pirates to the treasure—cleverly marked as "T" on his map—T for treasure!

Piddington told Pirate Petersen to steer the *Messi Sui* towards the tallest tree up ahead in the deepest darkest Peru, dock the fancy pirate ship and head out on foot.

The Tree of Rhythm stood out above the rest of the jungle. The Tree of Rhythm was actually a decoy. It was hard and fully dressed in vines. Cautiously, the pirate crew crept round the tree. All of a sudden, a giant dangerous vine monster headed towards the pirates at rapid speed, but the pirates chopped it with their swords. Immediately, the vines regenerated! The swords lost their sharpness because the vine monster had ruined them as they wrapped round the silver blades.

Piddington didn't expect to be a pirate without a sword!

Finally, after many attempts, they reached the Temple of Doom!

Dun dun duuunnn!

Standing at the top of the Temple of Doom was none other than the evil stinker himself, Mr Fart-Maker! Mr Fart-Maker had a clever trick—he put fake blood on his sword which scared people away! His rosy-red blade stood out against his shiny blue jacket. The same colours that Piddington wore. He thought he was way smarter than the pirates from Bruntsfield Pirate School. His number one aim was to defeat the Bruntsfield crew and overturn them. Once they felt the full force of defeat, Mr Fart-Maker would swoop in to the sound and smell of farts, turning the Bruntsfield crew into his army from strength to strength.

Mr Fart-Maker was farting into a number of balloons. His favourite thing was throwing delicious fart bombs and making a real stink.

Mr Fart-Maker wound up his arm. Round and round it went until finally... release! He let a fart balloon go, and Captain Hunt quickly whipped her deadly hair round to protect herself, but it hit Captain Hunt right on her nose! Captain Hunt collapsed into the lush, green leafy ground. She couldn't deal with toilet stench. She couldn't even listen to toilet humour!

The only thing that could save her from this smell coma was her loyal pal, Peck Peck.

Peck Peck swooped down from the canopies of the jungle and perched on her shoulders to flap the smell away from Captain Hunt's delicate nose.

Mr Fart-Maker returned and let out three more fart-filled balloons. Racing through the vines, the balloons flew as the smell spread out.

Fizzing through the air, the balloon had been repelled back and was aiming it directly at Mr Fart-Maker's smug face! Mr Fart-Maker ended up wrapped in the vines of the Tree of Rhythm. The vines held him tightly while the P3A crew and Piddington cheered and they continued their mission.

They climbed to the bottom of the Temple led by Iris, a future leader of the crew. She had sparkly, lime green hair and her blue eyes matched the colour of the ocean. Iris was fearless and could be trusted with any of Captain Hunt's duties.

The fellow pirate crew future leader was Harron. He had

dark brown hazelnut eyes, pitch black spikey hair and always carried a trusted sword as sharp as a sabretooth tiger's fang. His pirate hat with a skull and cross bones was never off his head. He couldn't even shower without it! In fact, he would faint if his pirate hat was removed.

Eventually, they got to the entrance of the Temple of Doom. *Dun dun duuunnn!*

Piddington led them straight to the spot marked "T" for treasure. This was the time where Piddington became crew member thirty-one of P3A!

Captain Hunt instructed Peck Peck to get Pirate King Grrrhooley on the Pirate Cam. "Grr grr, grr grr," echoed from the Pirate Cam.

Captain Grrrhooley answered with his usual, "Grr! Tell me you've located the treasure, me hearty Captain Hunt!"

Captain Hunt replied, "Aye aye, Captain! Take a look at our P3A crew mates at work." Captain Hunt turned the camera towards the digging crew.

Harron and Iris were digging furiously, but Kevin was sitting right in their way. Kevin was asked to move, but as per usual, he didn't listen! He was in the yellow zone and overly excited about the hidden treasure. As they were digging, they scooped mud, which hit Kevin square in the face.

Pirate King Grrrhooley smiled, and Peck Peck was quick to say, "In your face!" Pirate King Grrrhooley called out "Finally!" in a satisfied way. "I mean, finally Peck Peck can talk without mimicking!" he said as he looked down with a guilty face!

The treasure was retrieved with the help of crew member thirty-one, Piddington, and was returned to Pirate King Grrrhooley after the mammoth return journey home. Piddington had a feeling that something magical would happen with the treasure, but how would they ever find out?

P4A

8

RED HOT TREASURE

P4A

It was Wednesday evening and the ship's captain, White Bones, was helping scrape barnacles off the hull of the boat, getting it ready for its next adventure. Captain White Bones had a crew of thirty pirates. She had two heads, and they were always arguing.

Today, Captain White Bones was wearing a dark blue dress with a Bruntsfield badge on it. She had her short purple cardigan with patches sewn onto the elbows. Captain White Bones had one hooked hand and leather boots with gold rims. She always wore a flint lock pistol and a cutlass on her belt, and she loved throwing bombs. Her weakness was snake venom, so she tried to avoid the ship's mascot, Fang Tooth, as she was a bit scared of him.

Her pirate's ship was called the *Seven Seas*. It was huge at thirty metres long and twenty metres high, and it had been built in 1582. It was made from teak wood and was a shiny bronze colour. The ship's weakness would be a fire or a strong storm because it was so old. It had thirty-four fierce looking cannons (sixteen on each side and one at the front and back). The cannons were very heavy and were taller than the pirates.

The *Seven Seas* ship had three decks. The lower deck was where everybody slept—except for the captain, of course. It was cosy and dark down there. Sometimes the crew could see the sea creatures swimming at great depths through the cabin windows. The upper deck was where the pirates did most of their work. The captain had her own deck on top of the ship. It was where she could watch what is going on. She even had her own private toilet in her cabin. Captain White Bones also had lots of diamonds kept safely under her bed, but don't tell the crew! Her cabin was painted gold, and it was shiny in the sun. Captain White Bones liked playing darts when they were out at sea. She had the walls decorated with lots of paintings of all the previous captains, and she had lots of fishing rods so she could catch a tasty dinner for the crew.

The ship had a pirate boy called Chocolate Chip. His mum had given him this nickname, as he loved eating chocolate chip cookies so much. He was ten years old, and he was wearing his favourite blue and white striped t-shirt and bronze shorts. Chocolate Chip had a large pocket on his shirt with the letters "CC" written on it. This was where he kept all his cookies because he was always getting hungry.

Today it was his job to feed the ship mascot, Fang Tooth. Chocolate Chip liked looking after Fang Tooth. He was a green and yellow King Cobra snake with lots of lovely patterned spots on its back. He was fifty-six centimetres long, about eight centimetres wide, and he weighed around five pounds. Fang Tooth liked to curl up on the bottom of the ship's wheel to sleep. He liked eating pork, but he hated eating carrots. If Fang Tooth didn't like someone, his eyes would turn red. Long ago he was infected with a type of chemical, and it meant that his red eyes could freeze someone for twenty-eight days!

Scarlet was the ship's pirate girl. She was nine years old and had light yellow hair which was long and straight. She was thin and liked wearing her brown top and black skirt with the gold and black belt on it. Scarlet was wearing her new strong brown boots. She had a pet parrot called Jeff who liked to sit on her shoulder. Jeff was very colourful and wore his own little pirate hat. Today Scarlet's job was to help clean the rooms below deck. It was hard work!

The *Seven Seas* ship was in dock, and everyone was helping get it ready for its next journey. The crew were bringing food aboard, and Fang Tooth was resting in the crow's nest. People were guiding the cattle onto the ship with ropes and the water was being stored below deck.

Just then the pirate king arrived at the dock. He said, "Grrr," and stomped aboard the ship. The pirate king was called Grrrhooley, and he told the captain and crew that there was wonderful treasure hidden inside the Mount Etna volcano on the island of Sicily. "You are going to travel there to claim the treasure for me!" he said. All the crew were very excited, and they started making their preparations right away. The ropes were untied, and the ship started to set sail. Everyone waved goodbye as the ship sailed out of the dock toward their adventure.

On Thursday morning the ship was sailing on the calm water of the Mediterranean Sea. Chocolate Chip could smell the salt wafting from the sea. Scarlet was peering into the water, as she had noticed a shiny object under the waves.

Suddenly the ship started to shake, and the waves started getting rougher. A huge gloomy object emerged from the sea, and Scarlet's parrot Jeff flew away in fright. "Sea monster!" shouted Chocolate Chip.

The captain glared at it and reached for a bomb. It was a giant blue and green shiny sea snake. It had big fangs and scary red bloodshot eyes. Captain White Bones threw a bomb at the sea snake's head, and the snake was stunned for a moment. However, it spat venom straight at the captain. Unfortunately, this was the captain's weakness, and mid-argument both heads of the ship were knocked out.

Fang Tooth's eyes turned red, and he glared at the sea snake. The sea monster was frozen in the water.

The crew went as quickly as they could and jumped in the row boats. They paddled frantically to escape. It took them a few days of rowing to reach the island of Sicily. When they got close to the beach, they met a kraken called Smash and Bash. Smash and Bash was ancient—they had heard that she was over 400 years old. She was blue with red tentacles and looked quite cute when she first came out of the water. She gave the crew her best puppy eyes, and all the pirates looked over from the side of the rowboat and said, "Aww."

Scarlet told the crew that they weren't to be fooled by her cuteness because she had met Smash and Bash before, and inside, she was evil.

Smash and Bash started to grow into a giant monstrosity. She didn't like cleaning her teeth, and they looked horrible. The crew tried to row away as fast as they could, but something had caught the rowboat oars. "Oh no," they shouted. The rowboat was stuck, as they had been caught by one of Smash and Bash's large tentacles. They tried to turn the boat around, but Smash and Bash was too strong.

Scarlet was a quick thinker, and she pulled out her knife and cut off the tentacles that were holding them back. They were free again! Scarlet helped steer the rowboat back towards the beach, and they quickly found a good spot to row the boat up on to the sand.

When they got out, they all looked at the tentacles they had cut off. "Yummy," said Scarlet. They were all feeling hungry so Chocolate Chip suggested that they BBQ them. Everyone thought that was a great idea, so he chopped up the tentacles and grilled them. The smell of the fresh food made everybody even more hungry. "Calamari for everyone!" he shouted when they were ready. They each got two bits. They were crispy and appetising. "Thanks, Smash and Bash," said Chocolate Chip, and they all giggled.

When they were finished eating, they set off for Mount Etna. In the distance, they saw a white thing coming closer and closer towards them from the sky. Ten seconds later, Scarlet was completely knocked out by the white thing.

It turned out to be a football which had knocked her out. It had been kicked by Ronaldo the pirate. Ronaldo had been a famous footballer who had become a pirate when his leg was injured in an accident. He still had his short, spiky hair, and he liked putting lots of gel on it. He was wearing his old red and white football strip, but now it was ripped and tattered, and he had one wooden leg. It was his job to guard the treasure on Mount Etna. Ronaldo was very rich but not very fit anymore, and everyone hated him.

Chocolate Chip shouted at Ronaldo, and Ronaldo challenged him to a football match. He said that only the winner would be allowed to go inside Mount Etna. Poor Chocolate Chip stank at playing football, but he wanted to help the crew get the treasure. In the first half of the game Ronaldo had scored 100 goals and poor Chocolate Chip hadn't scored any!

At halftime Ronaldo was celebrating because he thought he was going to win. But then Chocolate Chip had a good idea. He gave Ronaldo a ginormous crate of cookies. Ronald had never had cookies before because he was so healthy. Once he started eating them, he couldn't stop. In fact, he ate so many that he started to feel sick and was getting bigger and bigger. He sat down by a tree for a rest. When the second half of the game started, Ronaldo struggled to play. Then he started to spew, and he couldn't play anymore. Chocolate Chip started scoring goals, and soon he had scored 101 goals, beating Ronaldo. "Hooray!" the crew shouted as Chocolate Chip had won the game.

The crew could see the volcano just behind the trees, so

they started walking quickly and quietly towards it. They thought they were being watched, so they went even quicker. Then they started running as fast as they could to the volcano. They spotted a small door at bottom of the volcano, so they went up and opened it. Behind the door there was a staircase. They went up the staircase, but one of the pirates stepped on a trap. Arrows started shooting out at them, so they ducked and ran up the stairs as fast as they could. At the top of the volcano there was another door. They opened it really quietly and tiptoed inside. There was a huge treasure chest inside the volcano.

When the crew picked up the treasure chest the volcano started to rumble. "Oh no, another trap!" shouted Chocolate Chip. They ran down the stairs carrying the treasure chest as fast as they could. They could see the lava was about to explode. They needed to get to the rowboat quickly. They passed Ronaldo who lying on the beach. He had got so round from eating the cookies that he looked like just a giant football. So, Chocolate Chip booted him as he ran past. Ronaldo flew up into the air and came down landing in the top of the volcano, plugging it like a cork. "Goal!" they all shouted! They ran back to the row boats laughing.

Scarlet had come to and was so pleased to see them with the treasure chest. "Let's get the treasure back to Captain White Bones and the ship. She will be so proud of us!" she cried.

So they too the treasure back to their captain, then to Pirate King Grrrhooley.

Epilogue: Twenty-five years later Ronaldo popped out from the top of the volcano. He had started to deflate and flew up in the air. He came down on the football pitch at the Champions League and scored the winning goal for Real Madrid. The crowd went wild!

P1C

9

THE ATTACKING BUMS
P1C

One sunny morning at Bruntsfield Primary Pirate School, P1C were reciting their diagraph sounds like any other morning. All of a sudden, Pirate King Grrrhooley burst through the door and handed Pirate NoNonsenseDogMcLeod a scroll with a ribbon around it that had just arrived in the post. The class were so excited and nervous to see what was inside the scroll.

When Pirate NoNonsenseDogMcLeod unravelled it, the class discovered it was a map. There was a giant X that marked the spot of buried treasure.

Together the class looked at the map and worked out where they needed to go. Using the clues on the map, they recognised it must lead them to Nepal, but it was not going to be easy for them to get there. They would need to go across many dangerous seas and pass the deadly sea monster. They decided the best and fastest way to get there would be to all jump aboard *The Dog Kennel*, their pirate ship, which was docked outside the school, and use their dog pirate skills to get there in one piece.

Before Captain Rosie left the classroom, she quickly

grabbed the class pet rabbits Dot and Honey. You never know, their special powers of spitting out carrots and jumping super high might come in handy. Dot and Honey were excited because they loved adventures.

The class all hurried to board the ship and got ready to set sail. Pirate NoNonsenseDogMcLeod was the captain of the boat and took charge of the steering. Captain Skull was in charge of holding the map to make sure they were going the right way. Captain Rosie was on the lookout for any trouble. Dot and Honey helped unravel the sail. Captain Rosie nodded at Pirate NoNonsenseDogMcLeod that the ship was ready, and together P1C started to howl. When they all howled together, it pushed the ship across the sea faster than ever.

"According to the map, we are nearly there!" shouted Captain Skull. The children all cheered, as it felt like they had been sailing the seas for 100 years. The class all let out a final howl, as they could see the coast in the close distance. However, Captain Rosie noticed something unusual. Out the corner of her eye, she thought she saw a giant bum splash in the water in front of them.

"Watch out!" shouted Captain Rosie as she watched a giant sea monster emerge out of the water. All the howling must have woken him up from his sleep when the boat passed by, and he did not look happy.

Children started screaming, as this was the biggest and ugliest sea monster they had ever seen. The sea monster had twenty heads, with 100 eyes, 100 legs and 100 bums. The sea monster leapt out of the water and landed on the boat. The boat swayed and slowly began to sink.

P1C had to think fast. Dot and Honey started shooting carrots out from their paws at the sea monster. Unfortunately, this did not work, as the sea monster loved carrots, and he started munching on them. When he had finished eating the carrots, the sea monster turned around and let out 100 farts from his 100 bums. Pirate NoNonsenseDogMcLeod did not like all this fart nonsense and fell to the ground. She was knocked out.

The class began to panic now that Pirate NoNonsenseDogMcLeod was down. Captain Rosie had an idea. She shot out 100 roses from her hands, one for each bottom so the monster could no longer fart. But the sea monster was still trying to fight the class by swinging around his tentacles.

Captain Skull stepped in and snapped his fingers to make 100 copies of Dot and Honey. Together, all the rabbits fired enough carrots to blast the sea monster back into the sea. The children watched as the sea monster sunk and disappeared out of their sight.

But suddenly, the sea monster popped back up, and the whole class screamed. Honey and Dot shot their last carrots right into the sea monster's eyes, and he exploded.

The whole class helped Pirate NoNonsenseDogMcLeod back up and got back on track to find the treasure.

The class were so relieved when they were finally in Nepal. One by one they jumped off the boat, ready to complete the last part of their mission. The sun beat down on P1C as they followed Pirate NoNonsenseDogMcLeod and Captain Skull using the map as their guide. As they turned a corner, they saw their pirate enemy—Captain Lost His Leg, who was looking for his missing leg.

"What are you doing here?" asked Captain Rosie, who was shocked to see him there.

Captain Lost His Leg let out an evil laugh and said, "Funny you should ask that. I am going to get the buried treasure!" Before the map had arrived at school, Captain Lost His Leg had a sneaky look at it and had a head start to find the treasure.

Captain Rosie and Captain Skull looked at each other and knew exactly what to do. Rosie blasted roses out of her hand to shock Captain Lost His Leg, and Skull snapped his fingers and made copies of the children in P1C.

Captain Lost His Leg was so confused that he started swaying. He got so scared that he cried like a baby and ran away.

Hoping that they wouldn't run into any more trouble, P1C quickly made their way to the temple at the top of the mountain. When they had finally arrived, they were sweaty and stinky from the hot sun beating down on them.

"That's where the treasure is!" shouted Pirate NoNonsenseDogMcLeod. The class all stood around the giant X in the garden of the temple, wondering what they should do next.

"We will need to dig for it," said Captain Rosie.

"Oh, I wish we brought our shovels!" moaned Captain Skull.

"Don't worry, we can just use our paws to dig!" answered Pirate NoNonsenseDogMcLeod.

Everyone worked hard to dig together until they found the treasure. "Hooray!" shouted the whole class. Dot and Honey gave them a thumbs up for all of their great teamwork.

Then they all went back to the ship and sailed to Pirate Bay. They proudly gave the treasure to Pirate King Grrrhooley.

P3C

10

THE BRUNTSFIELD PIRATES AND THE ATTACK OF THE SEA MONSTER

P3C

The P3C pirates were singing a joyful sea shanty when Pirate King Grrrhooley excitedly strutted along Bruntsfield Bay towards them. Pirate King Grrrhooley gave them their extremely hard mission, which was to find one of the twenty-one ancient and mythical pieces of treasure he was searching for. WOW!

P3C got packed up ready to set sail on their ginormous ship called the *Woodboard*, one of the twenty-one ships floating in the bay. The P3C pirate crew were led by Captain Iland, First Mate Sword Boy and First Mate Pirate Angel.

Everything went well until they met a gigantically huge, dangerous sea monster, who had a snake head, octopus's legs and a shark's body. ARGH! The sea monster was called Bob, and he started to attack them.

CRASH! BANG! WOLLOP!

Bob was, in fact, extremely shy and nervous and he was as quiet as a mouse, so that's why he attacked the pirates.

CBags and Laaamont, the two ginormous mosquitoes (the size of a laptop!) were flying around, and they accidentally flew into Bob's humungous creepy mouth! SPLAT!

When they got into Bob's tummy, they decided to tickle Bob. Bob laughed and threw up, and the two mosquitoes come out covered with banana gunk. BLARGH!

They both almost regretted tickling Bob's tummy because they were covered in gunk, and they both thought that banana gunk was gross! The two mosquitoes were revolted because they didn't like bananas. Luckily, however, Bob swam away.

Captain Iland, First Mate Sword Boy and First Mate Pirate Angel sorted everything out and the crew carried on with their exciting journey. While they were looking for the treasure, a ginormous amazing great white shark started following them without them realising. UH OH! Then some more sharks came, and the pirates still didn't notice!

After a few days, Captain Iland shouted, "Land ahoy!" HURRAY!

They landed at great, amazing Dubai and went to try to find the ancient mythical treasure. The pirates kept looking for the treasure using their big map, which was a large scroll. Eventually they spied something lovely and shiny which they followed in order to hopefully find the treasure... but it was only a shiny one shilling. BOO!

In the hazy reflection of the shilling, one of the pirates saw something coming behind them. It was a sandstorm. EEK!

"Aha my hearties, there's a sandstorm on the horizon!" one of the pirates said.

They hid quickly behind a palm tree to escape from the sandstorm. Unbelievably while standing behind the tree, they found the treasure! But hiding in the sandstorm was also evil Captain Skull, who had been close to getting the treasure for himself.

The sandstorm started to really get out of hand and sent the *Woodboard* crew and Captain Skull flying all the way on to the ship. THUD!

Captain Skull had some sand in his teeny tiny eyes, so his

vision was fuzzy. While he was trying to get the sand out of his eyes, the crew blindfolded him. The blindfold was very tiny.

The pirates forced Captain Skull to walk the creaky plank (he didn't want to, but he did because, well, he had to). This triggered a POOSPLOSION! KAPOW! The reason Captain Skull had a POOSPLOSION was because he couldn't ever go to the toilet ever since a great white shark had bitten his bottom. OUCH! Well, a POOSPLOSION was like when you pop a bag of crisps and all the crisps go everywhere... but it wasn't crisps, it was... YUCK!

The POOSPLOSION gave Captain Iland such a fright she tumbled overboard. SPLOSH! The great white shark that had been following the pirates opened its mouth and swallowed her.

Luckily Captain Iland got spat out by the shark because he didn't like the taste of Bruntsfield pirates.

Once back on board, the captain led her crew back to Bruntsfield Bay where First Mate Sword Boy and First Mate Pirate Angel handed over the unopened ancient and mythical treasure box to Pirate King Grrrhooley.

P6C

11

KRAKEN ADVENTURE

P6C

One perfect stormy, windy day at Bruntsfield Bay, the fearless pirates of P6C were ready to set sail across the seven seas to the Philippines. They were in their mighty ship called the *Crashing Cracker*. The *Crashing Cracker* was a massive wooden ship with enormous sails. It was very fast, yet it couldn't turn left because Hungry Jeff, the ship's pet who was a humungous walrus bird, ate the thingymajig that helped it turn left.

They were about to set sail to the Philippines to find one of the 21 treasures that were scattered around the world. Waves were smashing against the *Crashing Cracker* as all of P6C cleaned the ship to ready for an adventure.

The Pirate King, captain of all captains, Grrrhooley shouted, "Scrub the decks, hoist the sail, do this do that!" As everyone rushed off to work, he watched on with happy eyes until he fell asleep.

The boat's captain, Captain One Eye McL, was planning the route with the chief navigator Arrron. Arrron worked out that they were going to pass the bottom of South Africa and then sail onto the Philippines. What the captains didn't know was one of the ship mates had sneaked off before they set sail to order pizza and burgers.

Once they had departed they realised they had left one of their crew behind, SofAAARGGG, meaning she had to swim after them. Fortunately, a passing boat gave her a lift. The food was successfully sneaked on board, unseen by Pirate King Grrrhooley, and a secret party was held in the hold. Unfortunately, while everyone was eating the pizza and burgers, Hungry Jeff ate most of the ship's supplies, crackers and apple juice! It was too much even for a massive walrus bird, and he thew up the lot! Mr Grrrhooley and One Eye McL followed the smell and found the secret party.

Disaster! Mr Grrrhooley slipped in the sick and was so mad everyone was ordered back to work.

It was deckhand Oswimmer who sneaked the food on, so he was made to walk the plank. Luckily, as he had swimmer in his name, it turned out he was a champion swimmer and he swam to safety.

The rest of the journey was days of mopping, scrubbing and chores around the deck. As Hungry Jeff ate most of the food, they had to stop at South Africa to load up with more supplies. They tied him to the deck to make sure he didn't get into the hold again.

After the stop, they set sail and continued their journey towards the Philippines. The journey was uneventful with some minor issues until one day the ship started vibrating violently! There was a very unexpected visitor following them.

He emerged from the sea with sunglasses and a cap and started rapping:

I'm the Rapping Kraken Yo,
I'll eat you all like cookie dough,
And if you don't like that so,
I'll whip you with my humungous toe, YO!!

P6C started dancing to his catchy rhymes until somebody

realised what the lyrics meant. After some panic on board, Captain McL shouted, "Power up the engines, we will outrun this Rapping Kraken Yo!"

As they start moving, the rapping kraken started pushing the ship to the right towards the rocks. "Yo no," shouted AAArron, getting into the rap rhythm. "Remember we can't turn left, yo." The crew started panicking as they were heading full speed towards the rocks. What are they going to do?

Hungry Jeff had just finished his lunch of beans and was looking for a post lunch snack. He was flying around and spotted the Rapping Kraken Yo.

He licked his lips. Yummy.

Just at that point his beans hit his stomach, and he let out a mighty explosive *prrrrrrrrrrrrrrp*. The power of his *prrrrrrrrrrrp* launched the ship into the air, and it flew over the rocks and away from Rapping Kraken Yo!

When he realised what had happened, he dropped the ship back into the sea and landed with an almighty splash and soaked the crew. "Let him go!" shouted Pirate King Grrrhooley. The crew cut Jeff's ropes, and Jeff raced back to feast on the Rapping Kraken Yo!

Finally, thanks to Jeff, the journey continued peacefully, and they sailed on to the Philippines. They arrived on a beautiful day. The crew couldn't believe their eyes as they saw the glistening sands, golden beaches, tall palm trees and turquoise seas. They couldn't wait to get off to sunbathe and swim in the sea.

After an hour of lounging about, Pirate King Grrrhooley shouted for them to get back to work.

"Crew! Remember why we are here! Get back to work! Who has the treasure map?"

They quickly searched for the map, which one of the crew was using as a towel! Luckily, they could still read it. Moaning and complaining, they trudged off in the hot sun.

After hours of searching, they were starving. Suddenly someone shouted, "What's that smell?"

"Smells like bacon," said another.

They followed their noses and came to a clearing surrounded by trees. It seemed very pleasant, and best of all there was a big plate of bacon rolls in the middle. They all dashed towards the rolls to gobble up the bacon!

But it was a trap!

They were one bite in when a massive net was pulled all around them trapping them. Disaster!

Out of the forest came an evil laugh! Captain Chardeadbeard emerged from the bushes. They heard his evil laugh again, and he shouted, "Fools, you fell for my trap!" His minion pirates picked up the net and started to carry it away.

"Where are you taking us?" shouted Captain One Eye McL.

"They are taking you where no one will every find you," said Captain Chardeadbeard. The minions started moving the net and dragged it out of the clearing and dropped it in quicksand.

Everyone was shouting, screaming and panicking. "Shusssh," said someone as the net sunk deeper, "I hear something." They were all silent, and they heard the flapping of wings.

Hungry Jeff to the rescue again!

Their screams turned to claps and cheers. Hungry Jeff lifted the net and once again flew them to safety. As he was lowering them down, he lost his grip and dropped them right on top of Captain Chardeadbeard's beard. He was trapped under his own trap!

They continued on, following the map to the X. They came across a very unremarkable looking tree. It looked a bit dead, but it had two bits of fruit on it, an apple and a coconut.

Hungry Jeff pulled the apple from the tree to eat it, and a small door opened in the tree trunk! They peered in. "Hurrah!"

they shouted. "The treasure is here!" They pulled out a locked wooden chest. "We need to get this back to the ship safely," said One Eye McL. "Let's go."

They raced back towards the ship carrying the treasure chest. As they came to the beach, they noticed a cute pig coming towards them. They sniffed the air. They smelled bacon again. "Wait! It could be a trap again, get the nets," shouted one of the crew. They grabbed the net and threw it over the cute pig and carried him back to the ship too.

Pirate King Grrrhooley was waiting for them. "Great job crew," he said. "Now let's get out of here in one piece!"

They loaded the treasure and the pig onto the ship and set sail.

As they started sailing, Hungry Jeff suddenly noticed the pig. He sniffed.

"Uh oh," said Arrron, "I think he smells food." He raced towards the pig and got there just in time to rescue him from Hungry Jeff's clutches. The crew named the pig Patrick and decided to take turns to protect him from Jeff.

As they sailed back towards South Africa, they came across a small boat which Oswimmer was in! The crew begged Pirate King Grrrhooley to let him back on board, and he reluctantly agreed. Everyone was delighted to see Oswimmer. He had been drifting for weeks and was starving. He sniffed the air and smelt the lovely bacony smell of Patrick.

"Yum!" he said.

Hungry Jeff realised there was competition for the pig and ate Oswimmer!

"Oh no," said Captain Grrrhooley. "I'm going to have to fill out A LOT of paperwork when I get back to shore. "

The rest of journey home went smoothly and they finally spotted Bruntsfield Bay in the distance. There was a welcoming party of all the admirals—Wood, Lamond, Dobie and Nicol cheered as the crew raised the treasure chest to show them they had been successful.

When they docked, they unloaded the ship. "What are we going to do with Patrick?" said Captain One Eye McL.

That decision was taken out of their hands as the pig sprouted wings and flew away, with Hungry Jeff in hot pursuit, off into the sunset.

"Right," said Captain Grrrhooley. "Let's get this treasure back to the school."

"Aye aye, Captain!" shouted P6C.

P4B

12

ONCE UPON A TIME IN MADAGASCAR

P4B

Early one morning on July 26th the pirate class P4B set sail to Madagascar on the mighty *Speeder*. She was the fastest ship in Bruntsfield Bay that could outsail the fastest of rockets.

"Scrub the deck! We are nearly there! Come on!" demanded Captain Horntail McBain. The captain was a legend of the seven seas and was known for her loud deafening voice and strict personality. If someone for a moment forgot where they were and who they were dealing with and decided to ignore captain's order, she would widen her eyes of fire and flare her nostrils as if a puff of smoke was coming out of them. She would clap her hands strong enough to make a thunderous sound and then roar at the victim. She roared so loud that it rang in your ears several minutes later like a loud drum had exploded inside your head. The power of her voice would turn the waves around as if they were running for their life. All the crew in a flash would freeze in terror, hoping this time it was not for them. Sometimes the victim would just stand there gaping looking like poison had slowly paralysed their whole body. The rest of the crew were petrified. Eventually, the poor victim would faint, crashing to the ground, and would have to be dragged away from the deck, tied to the plank and left there until they come round again.

But that particular morning Captain Horntail McBain seemed to be in good humour, gazing at the wonderful grey clouds and revealing her toothless grin. She had a sweet tooth and did not make friends with the toothbrush, ever. She climbed to the crow's nest to study the map. The waves of the great Acacia Sea were building up height, and the clouds began to look much gloomier.

The first mates Hawk and Penny were arguing who should steer the ship. They kept on thinking that they were better than each other. Penny was beginning to realise that the ship was losing speed in the heavy headwind. Suddenly, there was a huge clap of thunder, and a flashing bolt came crashing down on the sea, missing the ship by inches. The unexpected noise made the captain drop the map. She jumped down from the crow's nest, catching the map in mid-air and landing on to the deck. She brushed herself down and said, "That was that!" hoping to get a round of applause. But there was only one clap —the clap of thunder! The thunder was even louder than the captain's voice.

The crew were minding their own business but then started to be covered in hailstones. The hailstones were getting bigger by the minute. The crew dropped their sponges and ran for cover. At that moment a large hail stone as big as a cannonball came crashing down on the ship, making a great hole. The waves started filling the ship with seawater. The crew were running frantically about. None of them knew how to swim because their swimming pool in Bruntsfield Bay was always out of order.

The only people left on deck were Captain Horntail McBain and the first mates. Penny and Hawk who were trying to control the ship by grabbing the steering wheel and pulling it in opposite directions—each one was trying to steer it in their own way. The ship started to tilt one way, then the other, until it almost capsized. The poor crew was swaying about in the hull trying to keep their balance while frantically splashing about in the almost infinite supply of water.

Soon the water level reached their chins. Penny and Hawk were pulling the wheel so hard that it snapped. The ship was now slowly sinking. The crew were screaming their heads off, terrified of drowning. But their luck was about to change.

The *Speeder* suddenly hit an underwater rock and snapped into pieces. The captain yelled, "Grab the pieces! Swim for your life!" They all doggy paddled to the shore. Luckily, at least they knew how to do that.

When they reached the shore, they were hungry and exhausted. One of the crew members was daft enough to chase a crab along the beach. The rest watched him thoughtfully, as he ran this way and that way, hoping to catch the crab. The crab scurried towards the captain who picked the crab up by its pincers.

"What is this place?" asked Captain Horntail McBain.

To her surprise the crab answered without a delay, "It is the mighty island of Madagascarrrrr. How are you daft enough not to know? Drop me now!"

"Well, fellow crab, thank you for the answer, but there is no need to be rude," said the captain.

"If you don't want to get washed away by the tide, come with me. I will show you the closest shelter where you can rest until tomorrow," replied the crab.

The crew followed the crab. Obviously, no one had ever told them that you should never trust a stranger! The crab led them to the mouth of a skull-shaped cave. The crab went into the cave, but the pirates couldn't follow it because it totally disappeared in the darkness.

"Come on in. It's really warm in here," called out the crab from the darkness.

"Yeh, but it looks very dark as well," replied the daft pirate.

"It's better than it looks," said the crab.

The pirates looked at one another and went in. The ground was uneven under their feet and something kept crunching with every step. It echoed as loud as the captain's voice as the crew stumbled in the darkness. Suddenly, the captain noticed a flicker of light. It was coming from the far end of the cave. The crew saw it too and all followed the captain towards the light. It turned out to be a torch fixed to the wall.

"Take this torch. You are going to need it," said the crab.

When the captain pulled the torch, the lights came on all around the cave. A part of the wall opened like a large door, and they heard a crashing sound. The entrance of the cave got shut tight. The pirates were trapped in the cave, fearing the worst. The ground was shaking and the crew could see the rising figures surrounding them. The figures had shark's heads and fins as well as human bodies and legs. The figures were the shark people. They started closing in on the crew.

"See you later," said the crab in a slightly creepy voice as it waved its pincers. "Or not! You are probably going to be dead soon. But don't worry, I'll come and visit your skulls with roses!"

The shark people led the crew through the tunnel to a large hole on the ground. They pushed the pirates into the hole. With loud cries the pirates descended to the depth of the cave, thinking they were going to die. Surprisingly, they landed in comfy chairs. The chairs were organised around a large dining table. The shark people came in from a side tunnel bringing bowls of soup with them. They placed the bowls on the table and invited the crew to eat.

The daft pirate said, "Ooh, I am very hungry! But I am a very fussy eater and I don't like soup. Please can I have some pizza maybe, with extra peperoni and no herbs, please?"

The shark people brought what he wanted and he scarfed it down whole. Penny scooped some soup with the spoon, smelled it and poured it back into the bowl. The soup smelled nice. She took another scoop and was about to pop it into her mouth when suddenly she spotted something white. She took it out and it happened to be a piece of a label with the word *Poison* on it.

"Stop eating everyone!" she screamed. "The soup is poisoned! So is the pizza!"

It was too late for the daft pirate. He already swallowed his pizza. He started running around the cave, screaming, "I'm gonna die! I'm gonna die!" Then, he suddenly froze and fell to the floor.

The crew stared at his body, stunned. The captain broke the silence.

"Well, that has sorted one problem. No more daft people!"

The shark people screamed at the chef, "You idiot! You left the label in the soup!"

"But I thought we didn't want them to die. They are nice pirates!" said the chef.

The captain threw her bowl of soup at one of the shark people. Her crew followed her example. Some soup landed on the floor, and some in the shark people's mouths. Immediately, the pirates rushed to the shark people and overpowered them. They tied shark people's fins and mouths with whatever they could find in the kitchen, like sausage strings. And the shark people did not dare to eat it because, just like every other food, it was poisonous.

"What shall we do with these shark people?" asked Hawk.

One of the shark people started pleading. "Don't kill us. We will do anything for you."

"Really? Anything?" said Captain Horntail McBain.

"Yes. We know where the crab is hiding his treasure!" said

the chef. He pointed at the stomach of one of the shark people. "The key is in there!"

The pirates rushed towards the shark person and pulled it to the ground. Hawk shouted, "On the count of three all jump onto the shark's belly! One, two, three!" The pirates jumped like on the trampoline.

The key went flying out of the shark's mouth and landed on the ground next to a small trap door. They used the key to open the trap door and saw a spiral staircase leading even further down. The sign on the wall said, **Danger! Traps may cause death!**

"I know what to do!" said Penny. She put on her headphones and started dancing.

"Not a good time for this!" said Hawk. But Penny ignored him and continued dancing down the stairs. Knives went out of the walls, arrows came flying from every direction, but she managed to dodge every weapon with her cool dancing moves. The last arrow came through with a key on it. She caught it quickly. It was the key from a treasure chest that stood at the bottom of the spiral staircase.

"Guys, I need some help here to move it up!" she shouted from down below. It was safe for the crew to go past because Penny has solved the traps and got the key. They all came to help.

With heavy puffing they brought the treasure up.

"What's the point?" said the captain. "We can't take it home. We have no ship!"

"Maybe we can ask the shark people to sail us home. They can swim!" said Penny. "And if they don't do it, there is still some soup on the table. We can feed it to them."

The shark people nodded their heads quickly. They didn't want any poisonous soup. The crew used the sausage strings to make reins for the shark people, mounted them and secured the treasure chest tightly on their backs. They did not forget their daft friend and strapped him onto the back of one of the sharks.

The fleet of shark people started swimming, but they could not gather enough speed. The captain had an idea. She went to the back of the shark people fleet and screamed. Her powerful voice moved the waves, and the fleet went speedily across the Acacia Sea. When the shark people felt the waves, they started kicking their legs even faster picking up more speed. In no time the crew reached Brunstfield Bay.

"What are we to do with shark people now?" asked Hawk.

"We can train them and keep them as eco-friendly boats. Or they can help us train children how to avoid the traps," said Penny.

As soon as they gave Pirate King Grrrhooley the treasure, that was the end of this adventure. The crew had organised for their daft friend to be a permanent exhibition at the National Museum of Scotland, a reminder to people of why it's important not to be daft when going on an adventure. And they lived piratly ever after.

As for the crab, he did visit the cave with roses, but he never found any new skulls nor did he find his way out of the cave again. Until this day, he scurries around the cave lamenting for his shark people, his treasure and the daylight.

P7A

13

FLUSHED AWAY WITH THE BRUNSTSFIELD BANDIT POTTY PIRATES

P7A

Midday sun beat down upon the harbour, and the flat, calm sea beckoned. However, all was not so restful aboard the ships moored there, as Pirate King Grrrhooley strode up and down, barking orders at everyone as the captains of the ship tried to dodge him.

Aboard the ship *The Golden Toilet*, skippered by Captain Toffee, already on her fourth cup of espresso, a young pirate girl, Azzurra Carozza, lounged lazily. She muttered insults to half of the crew, but mainly at poor Scrawny Joe. He busily did all of his work to prepare to set sail and half of Azzurra's too to keep her happy. An impossible task, he was quickly learning.

Squawking could be heard above all the other noises of the port, as Antigua, *The Golden Toilet's* parrot, flapped into view, missing a few tail feathers. His frenemy, Barbuda, the boat's Nile crocodile, slunk back behind a coil of ropes grinning, some brightly-coloured feathers sticking to his gums. The poor Hyacinth Macaw returned briefly to peck furiously at the nose of his crocodile foe, who was soon distracted once more by the sight of his glorious reflection in a mirror.

At last, the signal was given to cast off the ropes and set sail on their latest quest, which would take them thousands of miles across the Atlantic. They hoped! None of them were quite sure how they were actually going to get to California but were sure it would work out just fine. Pirate King Grrrhooley had ordered them to go in search of a very special box of treasure. He assured them this was the perfect mission for the crew of a ship named *The Golden Toilet*.

As the ship eased its way out of port, the local people of Bruntsfield Bay heaved a collective sigh of relief. The pirates made them plenty of money while in port, but the crew of the galleon *The Golden Toilet* were by far the worst. Lazy, smelly, noisy and useless! They were glad to see the back of them for a while.

Out with the calm of the bay, the first wave of any size had the ship lurching from side to side, such was the awful job they'd made of loading the food and equipment. This was enough to unsettle Antigua and Barbuda, who promptly started round two of their fight, due to the parrot being tossed onto the croc's head with the motion of the boat. Barbuda clearly saw this as a violent retaliation and lunged at the rowdy bird.

Heading southwards on the North Sea, a few uneventful hours passed and the pirate crew were feeling quite pleased with themselves.

"Ship ahead!" came a squeaky voice from high up in the rickety old crow's nest. It was Scrawny Joe on watch, clinging on for dear life. Directly in front of them was an oil ship, placing pipes on the sea bed. As the evening mist drifted, it became clear that several of these long ships formed a barricade. There was no way through.

Or was there?

Scrawny Joe reached for his emergency Irn Bru stash, the elixir of power for the scrawny boy. The "bravery bru"! Burping out the last of the bubbles, Joe leapt into the cold, grey water and swam towards the ships laying the pipes. Although his courage was strong, his body wasn't, and on reaching the first ship, he grasped the anchor chain, swung round and gave one of the lowering pipes one almighty kick as he screamed his battle cry, "SPINY SEA URCHINS!" He stubbed his toe. Whimpering in pain and shedding a tear, he then crawled up the chain and climbed aboard the huge, metal boat to challenge the crew.

"Move yer boat or get the beating of a lifetime," he warned, leaning forward, flexing his muscles and clenching his fists. At the sound of Joe's squeaky voice and the sight of his weak little body, the workers burst into hysterical laughter. Jamming a little kid's inflatable ring over his head, they grabbed Joe by his collar, and with his skinny limbs flapping and flailing wildly like a fish out of water, they threw him back into the cold North Sea.

"You'll regret this!" he squealed pitifully as he dropped. Humiliated, he doggy-paddled from within the *My Little Pony* ring all the way back to *The Golden Toilet*, trying to avoid the disdainful look on Azzurra's face. He was finally fished out of the water by Captain Toffee's granny, the oldest pirate on board, using her fishing rod. She pulled him out using only one hand, little effort and barely a bend in the rod, while Captain Toffee looked on proudly, downing her evening mocha and tickling the ship's cat under the chin.

As the rest of the clueless crew dithered, Azzurra took control. Cheese-obsessed and fed up with the time-wasting, Azzurra knew how to take the pipeline workers by surprise. Loading up the cannons with an array of out-of-date cheeses, (she would never use her good ones) she rallied some of the crew to fire at the boats ahead.

First to fly through the air was a lovely, big truckle of cheddar, solid enough to send Joe's oppressors into the stratosphere. A particularly smelly camembert (cannonbert!) pancaked its way towards the deck of the same ship, oozing large droplets as it flew and landed with a *poomph!* There it crept across the deck, bubbling and fizzing as it corroded the metal.

Next, straight from the fridge and hard as bullets, a barrage of Babybels was catapulted across the grey water and had the workers ducking for cover. Heat-ripened Gorgonzola that had sat in the heat of the galley for weeks had the workers holding their noses and retching. A brick-hard Pecorino knocked out the biggest and most muscle-bound of the men. A spray of grated Parmesan temporarily blinded those out on deck, and their calls of "Eat them to defeat them," was quickly ignored when the other workers realised just how rotten the cheese was.

Buffalo Mozzarella after Edam after Stilton hurtled onto the deck and into the hull of the boat. Giant globes of gouda were last, weighing it down so much that it began to capsize. The final one fell through deck after deck, with no one able to catch it. It blasted a hole in the bottom of the keel. In minutes, the ship had sunk to the bottom of the sea. The workers all grabbed the remainder of the embarrassing inflatables (they'd found a box of them floating from a ship that had lost some cargo), and with Joe's warning ringing in their ears, they paddled to safety in embarrassment.

Finally, as the final bubbles dispersed, a clear route appeared and *The Golden Toilet* began to glide smoothly through the gap with Azzurra shouting smugly from the stern, "Have a GOUDA DAY!"

As the Channel merged with the great Atlantic Ocean, the crew were completely unaware that they were being chased at full speed by "The Law". On an undercover jet ski powered by dolphins as a pirate called **Law**rence, he knew that this case—apprehending these filthy pirates—was his chance to shine.

Hot on their heels, the dutiful Law pulled up beside *The Golden Toilet* and called out for help.

Captain Toffee reluctantly rose from her bed, where she'd been lounging all afternoon reading a copy of *How to Make Your Cat Behave* and sipping on an Americano, when Scrawny Joe announced they had a new pirate on board. Rolling her eyes at the intrusion, she shuffled out to meet him. To her surprise, the "new pirate," who claimed to have been shipwrecked and now lost, had already made himself useful. Rather than having to learn the ways of the ship, he had everything shipshape! He'd plotted the route, given everyone useful tasks to do and set the sails just right to make the most efficient use of the wind and befriended everyone.

"OK, he's a keeper," nodded Captain Toffee, and she shuffled back to her cabin to resume her important work of the day.

While the crew were feeling confident that their trip was now going to be a success now that there was a new pirate, Antigua and Barbuda kicked off again. With the course set and Joe at the helm, the animals began fighting over who was the favourite of the new pirate. Joe was used to such fights, so turned his attention to Azzurra. Would she ever notice what a worthy pirate (and boyfriend) he could be? he wondered. Distracted, he took his eye of the ship's wheel. Slowly, slowly, the vessel began to veer off course and was soon heading in a north-westerly direction. Of course, the now hard-working crew didn't notice a thing. Captain Toffee was now fast asleep, an achievement in itself given the ridiculous amounts of coffee she'd consumed.

After drifting for some hours into the night thinking they were making good progress, the night watch retired to their hammocks to warm up. The day watch was surprised at the temperature, which had plummeted to -5 C. Before long, ice crystals had formed on their hair, eyelashes and eyebrows. Azzurra's nose was bright red at the tip, which Scrawny Joe found adorable, and some of the pirates sported beards that had turned the same shade as Santa's in the frosty air.

Well-rested and in a rare cheery mood, Captain Toffee breezed onto the deck with her breakfast cappuccino and Antigua perched on her shoulder.

The cheeky bird was calling, "Boss is coming. Warning! Warning! Swab the decks. Hoist the sails!" Barbuda crept out from under the ropes and reached towards the macaw, widening his jaws in his own warning.

"WHAT ON EARTH...!" began Captain Toffee, her entire body and coffee cup shaking with rage. Barbuda skulked of towards the plank, preparing to walk off it into the Arctic Ocean as a better option than what was to come! Everyone else froze.

"You incompetent rascals, I didn't ask for iced coffee. WHO has steered my ship into the middle of a DEEP FREEZE? This is outrageous, you intolerable smoothbrains!"

Antigua chattered unhelpfully in the background, "Oooh, someone's in trouble. Who's a naughty boy? Who's a naughty boy?"

Shielding their faces, the crew gave nothing away. Slowly, Scrawny Joe began sliding, against his will, across the deck, towards the captain, as if admitting guilt. The others followed, as they realised the bow of the ship was being lifted. Ice beneath the surface of the sea was levering the boat up at one end with a chalkboard screech.

"STEER US OUT OF HEEEEEEERE!" bellowed Captain Toffee. All hands scurried towards the ship's wheel, but they were too heavy-handed. Under the pressure of so many frantic hands grasping and pulling, the wheel broke off and landed in bits on the icy deck.

Red with rage, Captain Toffee was silenced when "The Law" sprang into action, quickly cobbling together the pieces of wood in a make do and mend fashion. Using some rope and clever knots, he saved the day with a functioning, if not very pretty, ship's wheel.

Still balanced on the ice, the captain had a plan.

Bursting into her cabin and through to her en suite, Captain Toffee prepared to reveal her best kept secret. The golden toilet that lay behind the door was encrusted with diamonds, rubies, sapphires and emeralds. Gazing in awe, the pirates thought it must be terribly uncomfortable to sit on. They realised, of course, that none of them had ever been asked to clean it. Given that the captain never lifted a finger to do any work herself, it would seem she didn't trust them to be anywhere near her precious loo.

What happened next shocked them all.

Pressing an elaborate combination of the jewels, the golden toilet began to rise and open, revealing a hi-tech arrangement of equipment that wouldn't have seemed out of place at NASA. Jaws dropping, the pirates were left thinking, *Why have we been putting up with such appalling conditions on this miserable ship while she's been hiding this? No TV, a rubbish cooker and a cold dribble of a shower with a torn curtain out on deck!*

Looking like they wanted to stage a mutiny, Captain Toffee knew she had to act quickly. "Joe—hop over here and press the giant, flashing red button. Azzurra—get out on deck and steer us out of this perishing place."

Azzurra, as usual, was quick on her feet at the helm in no time. Nervously, Joe edged forward, finger hovering hesitantly over the button. "NOW!" shouted Toffee. Joe slammed his hand down onto the button in fright.

The ship took off from the iceberg and barely skimmed the surface of the water as the rocket-like engine was activated. Flames shot out the back, melting the giant iceberg and raising the sea level a smidge! Reaching Mach 10, the hypersonic ship hurtled southwest towards the Caribbean Islands, the faces of the crew distorting with the force. Again, they thought to themselves, *Why have we been hoisting sails and doing everything by hand when we had all this tech hiding on the ship?*

Slowing to sail power only and peeling off layers as they approached the warm Caribbean waters, the captain wanted to make sure they didn't draw too much attention to themselves. They were now in prime pirate-infested territory. The *Black Pearl* glided by ahead of them, playing, *doo doo doo doodoodoodoo doo doo doo.*

Toffee rolled her eyes and muttered, "Jack Sparrow—enormous show-off."

They sailed happily to San Francisco, and as they turned into the bay, their usual plan to conceal their true identity came into play—boards and banners advertising the ultimate tourist experience on a replica pirate ship! Waving cheerfully to passers-by as they moored their boat near Redwood City, they made sure their "closed" sign was up.

Transport was required to go in search of the treasure, and Antigua was on the case. Having carried out a reconnaissance mission of the area and snacked on the cheese and tea, he left a helpful poop trail for the pirates to follow, all the way to the Flying Car Showroom. Inside, an auction was underway. Fascinated, the captain pushed her way to the front and, to everyone's surprise, started bidding! They were PIRATES! What was she doing? They busied themselves with taking one of the other cars WITHOUT paying for it and hoped she didn't get too carried away. Just as they had released the flying car from its podium and disabled (smashed) the alarms, they managed to get it airborne just as they heard the auctioneer call, "SOLD! To the lady in the pirate hat."

Soon they were hovering over Cupertino and the Apple Park in their new car. Within lay the treasure. At that moment, the technological wonder that was the flying car ceased to be a wonder as the fuel tank registered EMPTY, and it plummeted towards the ground, smashing through the shiny glass roof of

Apple Headquarters. The weight of a 700kg panicking crocodile didn't help matters. Security came flying through every door and head of security, Jeff, immediately recognized "The Law" and said loudly, "Hey my old pal, have you come all the way over from Britain to help us arrest these crooks?"

All pirate eyes glared at "The Law," who now had his chance to be recognized by his bosses. To take credit for punishing piracy. But he paused. He looked into the eyes of each and every one of the pirates and realised something. He realised he didn't want to lock them up. He realised he'd never enjoyed himself as much as he had since he set foot aboard *The Golden Toilet*. He realised he wanted to be a pirate and live a life of adventure at sea. He simply answered, "Not today, Jeff," then with an ear-splitting roar, he and the other pirates charged at the guards, while Barbuda wandered amongst them gnashing his yellow teeth and Antigua boxed them about the ears with his madly flapping wings. Azzurra set upon them with some radioactive-looking, processed cheese slices, slapping them around the cheeks.

Scrawny Joe sneaked off to locate the treasure. People underestimated him, but he wasn't as daft as they thought. Heading down to the Apple vault, he quickly turned back, as he needed the toilet. An empty loo roll hung and he scrambled around in a cupboard for a new one. Behind the stacked rolls was an unassuming, flattish box. Some strange-looking cotton balls sat nestled on top. Picking them up, he saw something move.

SPIDERS—his worst nightmare!

Dropping them to the ground, he ran away, whimpering.

But just then Captain Toffee arrived. She kicked the hatching spider eggs to one side and in doing so discovered a plain, grey box. She knew at once what it was. The treasure they had been sent to find.

Typical, Captain Toffee thought to herself, *that it was to be found in a toilet!* Pirate King Grrrhooley would, no doubt, laugh himself silly at that!

She held the plain, grey treasure box aloft and sighed, "Not a bad week at the office!"

They returned to Scotland to deliver the treasure to the pirate king.

PiB

14

THE PIRATES OF P1B
P1B

The *Skeleton Ship* of Primary 1B waited at the harbour of Edinburgh right next to the king's boat. The king didn't like the *Skeleton Ship* because it smelt terrible. As we know, the king does not like smelly things.

The red flag flew over the boat with its skull and cross bones. In the *Skeleton Ship,* there were round windows and square windows but just one toilet. This toilet smelt awful. In fact, it smelt like rotten pants and rotten orange skins! The boat's sail was gigantic and white and blew in the thin wind. The rusty red and black wood creaked as the craft gently rocked from side to side. There was a life boat if they sank. But nobody wanted to be saved with it because it smelt awful like the toilet!

Canons peeped from the sides of their ship. There was even a knight that guarded the top deck. The pirates of P1B were defending it from the terrible pirate Spike Sauce.

The crew of the ship, the pirates of P1B, were really called the Black Killer Whale Crew. The crew had a special jewel room where they kept their treasure. Unfortunately, the room was completely empty. Well, there looked like there was one jewel there, but in fact it was actually a very still spider. In the room there were plenty of traps. Boulders might swing and knock you down. There were also flying swords!

Stairs led down to the basement of the ship where you could find a small café that sold fish and chips. They had barrels of fish, water balloons and cannon balls down there too.

The crew slept in the middle of the ship in bunk beds. The bedrooms had portholes and hammocks.

Captain McFarsand had a room all to herself. She had a guard dog called Shiny who slept at the door.

The pirates of PiB gathered in the belly of the ship to think about the problem of the toilet. They had no money to get the toilet fixed as all their treasure has been taken by Spike Sauce.

"We could get the spider to unblock the toilet?" suggested Treasure Shine.

"No no no, that won't work" said Turtle 2. "We should all just get jobs. We're at the docks, so why don't we join a fishing club?"

Suddenly Pirate King Grrrhooley burst in. "Good morning everyone, I have some good news! You are saved! I have heard this very morning that there is treasure buried in a cave in Sweden. The deep dark cave of Norway! But there is just one problem… you will have to beat Spike Sauce to the treasure."

"Here is the map… good luck everyone!" Mr Grrrhooley exclaimed as he disappeared from the room through an open porthole.

All the crew began to cheer. "We can fix the toilet using the treasure. We will sell the gems for money and then we can get a new toilet!" cried Mr Moonsand!

"But remember," warned Captain McFarsand "We will still have to get to Sweden before Spike Sauce."

Spike Sauce was a very messy pirate. He had sauce all over his face. He had brown bedraggled hair with a red hat. He loved treasure and was very very nasty.

The crew looked at the map given to them by Pirate King Grrrhooley. On the map they found a giant sea. The sea was full of dolphins, sea horses and seals. But in the deepest darkest section of the sea lurked sharks and the dreaded Titan monster.

The crew of the *Skeleton Ship* set sail on the sea. The day was clear and the sea was soft. But as soon as the boat entered the deep water, a stormy wind began to howl. Suddenly a head came slowly out of the choppy water. Its black eyes stared straight at Captain McFarsaand. Its head was a disgusting dark green colour and its octopus arms began to drift towards the boat. Then came the dreaded flipper claws.

"Get the net!" shouted Turtle 2.

The crew threw the net onto the monster, but it snipped the net in half with its claws and began to climb aboard the boat.

"Fire the canons!" cried Treasure Shine. The first canon ball was eaten by the beast and the second fired into its slimy eye. The monster fell off the ship and onto the pointy rock in the middle of the stormy sea. It turned flat as a pancake because all the air escaped from its body.

"Yeeeeeeeeeeeeeeees!" shouted the crew. Everyone was so happy. But then they smelt the terrible barbeque sauce smell that could only mean that Spike Sauce was near. They turned and saw Spike Sauce's ship on the horizon. The crew fired the canons and shot arrows at Spike Sauce's ship, and he finally fell in the water.

The crew sped away using their giant emergency propeller. Behind them, Spike Sauce clambered back on his boat and followed the *Skeleton Ship* to the land.

The ship arrived at the shore of Sweden at the same time as Spike Sauce. There was a massive rock on the beach, and the crew knew that the cave of Norway was nearby because it was on the map.

The pirates tried to get past Spike Sauce, but he threw down some of his terrible sauce. Turtle 2 slipped in the sauce and fainted, becoming terribly sea sick. The rest of the crew tiptoed carefully round the sauce. Treasure Shine threw water on Spike Sauce, which melted the rotten sauce away.

Behind the beach lay a large dark forest. They walked into the forest and saw a bear watching them. The crew darted into a tunnel which appeared before them. They walked through the dark, dark tunnel. In the tunnel there were bats and spiders everywhere. Mr Moonsand scared the bats away by playing a terrible noisy song on his guitar.

At the end of the tunnel there was a large rock like the one on the beach. Captain McFarsand caught a strange golden spider and put it on the rock. The spider unlocked the rock and it broke apart. At the top of the rock there was a special compartment and a glowing key. Mr Moonsand used the key to open the compartment. There the pirates found a wooden box as big as a chair. It had stars carved into the wood. From underneath the lid glowed a beautiful light.

"This must be the treasure!" the crew cried.

The pirates of P1B rushed through the tunnel carrying the chest between them. As they entered the forest they found Spike Sauce wandering about. He spotted them. The crew sprinted to their ship as Spike Sauce ran after them. Shiny the dog leapt from the boat and growled and barked like a lion. Spike Sauce screamed and ran off. He was terrified of dogs.

The crew managed to get the treasure back to the special jewel room. As they laid the treasure chest down and caught their breath, they realised it had another smaller box inside it.

"I'm sure this is going to be enough treasure to fix the toilet!" said Captain McFarsand excitedly. "But this other small gold box we must take back to Pirate King Grrrhooley to open."

And so the *Skeleton Ship* set off back through the seas to Edinburgh. When they arrived, they gave the small gold box to Pirate King Grrrhooley.

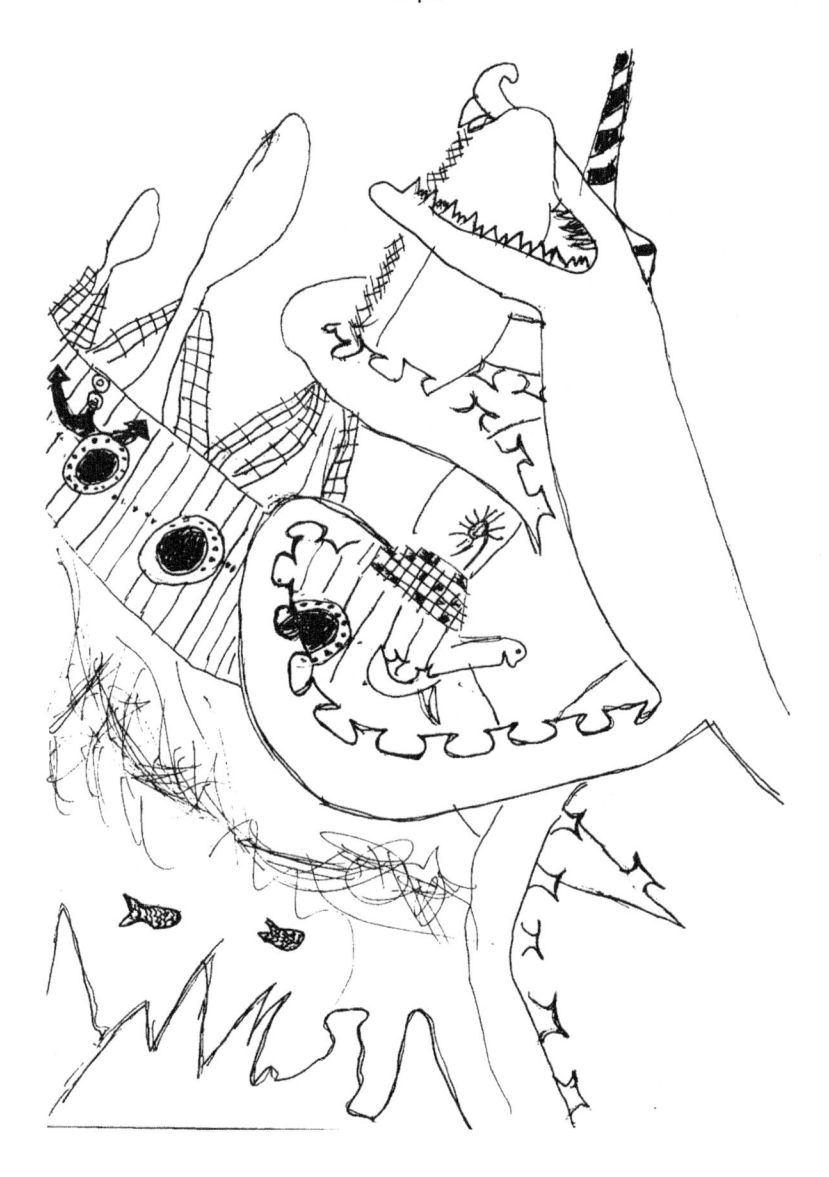

P4C

15

THE BILLY OF TEA AND FEROCIOUS FIN

P4C

It was a beautiful sunny day, and *The Billy of Tea* (the fiercest ship around) was docked at Pirate Bay. The crew were busy at work: Captain Pegleg was peeling bananas for lunch (her favourite food); Tom (the first mate) was chasing mice around the ship while Hedi scrubbed the poop deck. The rest of the crew were busy making cannon balls in case they ran into any trouble.

All of a sudden, Pirate King Grrrhooley sprinted onto the ship screaming at the top of his lungs, "I found a map and it shows me where Ferocious Fin has hidden his ancient treasure. It is in a fish market in Hong Kong!"

The crew gasped in shock and delight! Ferocious Fin's treasure was famous around these parts, but until now, nobody knew where he had buried it!

Immediately, Captain Pegleg started shouting orders at her crew to set sail while she studied the treasure map. They wasted no time in preparing the ship, and within a few minutes *The Billy of Tea* was well and truly on its way. Excited and joyful, the crew sang and waved goodbye to land.

Little did they know what danger lay ahead.

For several hours the ship sailed without any problems and everyone was joyful, but Tom knew this couldn't last. Carefully and nervously, he climbed up to the crow's nest and looked out across the water. Almost immediately, dark clouds started rolling in towards the ship. All around, Tom noticed the water had turned black as big waves started to form in the distance.

Something was wrong.

Without warning, the most frightening monster Tom had ever seen erupted from the water. It had the body and head of a crocodile, but where it should have had legs and arms, instead this monster had long orange tentacles and a giant horn protruding from the centre of its head. The monster was angry, and it furiously started to attack the ship.

Instinctively, the crew started to fire cannons at the monster, but it was no good! It was too strong. Captain Pegleg sprinted to her cabin to look up her book of mythical creatures. Frantically, she flicked through the pages until she finally found what she was looking for. The monster was a croctopus! As she continued to read, the captain let out a small shriek of laughter as she couldn't believe what she was reading; the croctopus was highly allergic to… bananas. As fast as her legs could carry her, she ran back to the crew to tell them what to do.

At the top of her lungs, Captain Pegleg told her crew to load up the cannons, not with cannon balls but with the bananas she had peeled earlier on in the day. Confused but desperate, the crew did as they were told and very quickly the cannons were ready to go.

"On my orders… ready, steady, FIRE!"

The bananas flew out into the sky like mini yellow rockets and hit the croctopus's head, body, face, eyes and some even flew directly into his mouth. Instantly, the croctopus started to sneeze. He made the loudest noise any of the crew had ever heard. He sneezed and sneezed and sneezed until he sneezed so much that the force of the sneeze caused him to blast off the ship back into the open ocean. Terrified, the croctopus knew he had been defeated and swam as fast as he could away from *The Billy of Tea*, never to be seen again!

The crew, who were now covered in bananas, hugged each other and jumped up and down in happiness. "Three cheers for Captain Pegleg," exclaimed Hedi, and she ate some of the banana that was squashed onto her arm.

The Billy of Tea continued to sail safely for the next few weeks as it got closer to Hong Kong. However, just before the ship reached land, it had an unexpected visitor in the middle of the night. As the crew slept soundly, Ferocious Fin crept onto the boat and into the captain's room. Ferocious Fin was a very strange man indeed. He mostly looked like a human, but he had a large shark fin on his back and inside his body was not one stomach but four (just like a cow). Just as Fin was about to reach out and kidnap the captain, a loud screeching sound erupted around the ship, waking up everyone, including the captain.

Out of the night sky, the most amazing bird-like animal appeared and bit Ferocious Fin on the bottom, causing him to slip on a banana skin and fall out of the boat and into the sea. The creature was very like an eagle (with wings and claws) but had the face of a wolf and had made the noise that had woken everyone up. The creature, called Sharky, had been sent by Pirate King Grrrhooley to help save the crew when they needed it.

Once everyone had calmed down, *The Billy of Tea* continued to sail towards Hong Kong; the treasure was getting closer. A few hours later, the ship docked, and the crew excitedly jumped out, causing the poor citizens of Hong Kong to run and hide. Unfortunately, Captain Pegleg's crew didn't notice the strange man with an unusually large humped back running off ahead of them.

For several hours, Captain Pegleg, Tom, Hedi and the rest of the crew followed the map towards the fish market. It was a long and tiring walk, but they knew the treasure would be worth it! Finally, the crew arrived at the abandoned fish market. It was a large building filled with glass boxes that contained dead rotting fish. The rotting fish smell made all the pirates gag, and some of them even fainted and fell dramatically to the floor.

Once everyone was on their feet again, they made their way towards the basement where they knew they would find the treasure.

Down towards the basement the crew followed their captain nervously. As they entered the dark and dingy room, they saw, in the middle of the floor, exactly what they were looking for. "Well, that was easy!" exclaimed Hedi as she walked towards the treasure chest. But no matter how hard she tried, the chest just would not open.

Every member of the pirate crew tried, but the lid simply wouldn't budge. Unexpectantly, out the darkness, Sharky flew through the air and pooped on Hedi's shoulder. "Eeeewww," she cried before she noticed something gold sitting on her shoulder.

It was a key!

Excitedly, Hedi ran towards the treasure chest, inserted the key and lifted up the lid! Instantly, the room was flooded with terrifying zombie fish! The zombie fish were completely see-through, but their razor-sharp teeth were definitely real! The crew ran frantically around the room as the fish tried to bite them. But then more danger appeared: Ferocious Fin jumped out from his hiding place, opened his giant mouth and swallowed Captain Pegleg whole!

Everyone started to scream and shout, but Tom kept calm and came up with a plan. Carefully he dodged the zombie fish and managed to find Hedi in all the commotion and explain to her what she needed to do.

Frantically, Hedi ran to the front of the room and started to dance. She waved her hands in the air before spinning around of the floor. The rest of the crew understood the plan and started to show off their best moves.

Amazingly, their dancing was so good and the zombie fish were so mesmerised, as was Ferocious Fin, that everyone started moving and grooving as well. But Tom was not distracted. As Ferocious Fin started to slide across the floor, Tom poked him in the bottom, causing him to jump, scream and sneeze.

Captain Pegleg came flying out of Fin's mouth and landed on the floor completely unharmed. In that moment, Hedi grabbed the treasure chest, Tom grabbed Captain Pegleg, and the whole crew ran back to *The Billy of the Tea* as fast as they could. Ferocious Fin and the zombie fish tried to follow the pirates, but they were too tired from all their dancing and very quickly gave up.

Once *The Billy of Tea* was safely sailing towards Pirate Bay, the crew all burst into spontaneous laughter. "I'm so happy we are all safe. Even if I did get eaten by a man with four stomachs," explained Captain Pegleg. "It was all worth it in the end!" Captain Pegleg placed the treasure chest safely under her bed.

Once they returned to Pirate Bay, the captain proudly gave Pirate King Grrrhooley the treasure.

P7C

16

PIRATE ADVENTURE

P7C

One day by the edge of Bruntsfield Pirate Bay, Pirate King Grrrhooley, handed the great Captain Seakane a map and wished him good luck on his voyage. Pirate King Grrrhooley asked him to return with any treasure of his own choosing but more importantly with a secret locked box which could only be opened by him.

All the people of the bay had a big parade and cheered Captain Seakane down the streets. There was singing and dancing. To be honest, the boat was only two minutes away, but it was a truly fun two minutes.

Captain Seakane had an octopus on his shoulder. The octopus was his best friend and his pet. Captain Seakane thought it was better to have an octopus instead of a parrot for multiple reasons, but he liked it mostly because it had eight arms and was great at multitasking.

He invited both his first mates, Tom and Lily, to join him on the voyage.

At last, they saw the mighty beautiful ship, the *Harbinger of Death*. Captain Seakane stroked his beard with a smile and walked towards his good old ship, exclaiming, "Hello, my old beauty, long time no see!"

The journey went well until Tom spotted a glowing wall that stretched across the horizon. The closer they got, the taller the wall seemed until it loomed over them, making the ship look tiny.

The sea started to get more treacherous, and the captain shouted, "It's starting to get hard to steer the ship," as his face went red with concentration and terror. The crewmates gasped with fear. Just at that moment, an enormous wave hit the ship, and it veered straight into the mysterious wall. Someone on the deck screamed, "It's SEAWEED!" as the glowing tentacles reached out.

The ship was rocking wildly from side to side, and just at that moment, the captain's pet octopus fell from his shoulder and into the water with a splash. The octopus started eating the seaweed and was growing at an alarming rate. Soon the octopus was big enough to smash the wall in half, creating a clear path for the *Harbinger of Death*, which sailed through as the octopus swam beneath it.

Captain Seakane and his crew made it to the island, but the crew realised that the captain was worried. They feared for him and questioned his decision. He grunted loudly and his eye twitched. They tried to continue the conversation, but he seemed eager to end it hastily.

The crew bounded off the plank and landed on the island. It was eerily silent. The sun seemed like their only companion. They took a few steps forward. Still no sound. A seagull flew by and squawked in terror as a singular rubber band shot through the thick air behind it.

Panic spread through the crew. They weren't alone.

Suddenly, something moved in the bushes ahead. Then a substantial sweaty red nose emerged from the foliage. Soon, the rest of the face followed. His beard was knotted from seawater and rubber bands. He had rubber band earrings, a rubber band eyepatch and a rubber band tunic. A menacing sight!

Captain Seakane's knees knocked against each other in distress.

It was Big Jones!

"Well, well, well," Big Jones smirked as he swaggered forward, a playful expression on his face. "What do we have here?"

He looked at each one of the pirates, most of whom shivered under his cold, powerful gaze. A hamster emerged from his breast pocket and growled at them with his small face.

"Who wants to kiss my blade?" he said as he drew his cutlass and light sparked off it. It had a rubber band hilt, a rubber band cross guard, and only the blade was silver mixed with amethyst.

Despite his fear reaching everywhere inside him, Captain Seakane stepped up and said defiantly, "Go and kiss your own blade, if you love it so much."

"Oooooh, burn," the crew said.

Big Jones growled and leaped at Captain Seakane, his sword a blur in the air, and Captain Seakane dodged at the last second. The evil pirate barely managed to regain balance. Captain Seakane drew his own cutlass, and both pirates started a duel, insulting each other at the same time.

Finally, after what felt like hours, Captain Seakane landed a blow on Big Jones, which resulted in a thin but long cut on his arm.

They had a few crucial moments, and the captain and his crew got away. They trudged up to the centre of the island where the tallest tree stood.

"I don't see any treasure," said Lily, clearly frustrated.

"That's because it's hidden," retorted Tom. They searched all around the tree and shook every branch until all the coconuts were on the ground. They split every coconut trying to find a key, until there was one coconut left. They cracked the last coconut and inside there was... another coconut! So they cracked that coconut, and inside that coconut was a key!

Tom climbed back up the tree and Lily scampered around in the roots, both looking for a keyhole.

"This is hopeless," sighed Lily after a while, sitting by the tree.

Suddenly there was a mechanical groaning noise, and one of the roots lifted into the air.

"You're a genius, Lily!" cried Tom as he scampered down the tree to put the key in the keyhole that was under the root. A trapdoor opened to reveal the greatest diamond they had both ever seen and a small, locked box. They grabbed the diamond and the box together and started walking back up the hill with Captain Seakane and the crew. The hill overlooked the port where the *Harbinger of Death* was moored. They were oblivious to the fact that Big Jones was slowly walking up behind them.

The three pirates reached the peak summit that overlooked the docked *Harbinger of Death,* still holding the diamond and box in their arms. A loud yell projected behind them. Captain Seakane's eyes went wide. "By the beard of Davy Jones, is this real?"

A breathless sound echoed behind them, and the scraping of metal sounded. "Ya hav' tak'n that diamond," Big Jones said, still wincing from his cut earlier, "but ya won't survive ta see yar island again."

"Oh, please," Tom said.

That was it. Big Jones, red in the face, his beard almost smoking, charged forwards with his cutlass. Tom drew his own.

Tom was struggling against Jones' heavy strikes. Lily, on the other hand, ran down the hill with the diamond and the small treasure box and hid them on the ship.

"Go Tom!" Captain Seakane shouted, attacking Big Jones himself. "GET TO THE SHIP!"

As if on cue, Big Jones knocked out Captain Seakane and dragged him towards his rubber band catapult, which would undoubtedly kill the captain.

"NO!" Tom shouted as he raced towards the captain, but he was thrown back by the punch aimed at his head. Lily returned up the hill to Tom.

"We must help him..." Tom managed to say before he passed out.

"We will, but we need a plan," Lily said before carrying Tom back to the ship.

"What will we do?" one of the crew asked.

"How will we win?" another said.

"We've lost."

"We haven't lost," Lily said firmly, propping Tom gently against the stairs and wrapping a cloth around his head. "We just need a plan."

The crew started pondering on this.

"Blow Big Jones up with the cannons?"

"We risk killing the captain."

"Destroy the island?"

"Same outcome."

"I could play the organ."

"HOW DOES THAT HELP?!"

"Sorry," the pirate said and sunk back into the crew.

"Wait," a groggy Tom said, blinking his eyes. "How about we pretend to give ourselves to Big Jones and rescue the captain from his grasp?"

A murmur fell over the crowd.

"Sounds crazy."

"We *are* crazy."

"Sounds good."

"I'm sold."

"Right," Lily said, like the captain of the ship. "So we give ourselves to Big Jones and then we knock him out, tie him to his own rubber band catapult and after we save the captain, we go and launch Big Jones into the ocean, never to be seen again. Yup, crazy, but we *are* crazy."

A hush then fell over the pirates. Lily, starting to get impatient, shouted, "Off with it, ya scallawags! Ya dirty dogs! Move!"

The climb up the slope was tiring but worth it as they saw the rubber band catapult.

"Wait!" Lily cried. Big Jones was about to launch the catapult, but Lily's cry stopped him. Small Jones, his hamster, looked at her in disgust.

"What, ya little girl?" Big Jones sneered. "I'm about to throw your captain into the sea."

"Well," she said smoothly. "We want to be your crew since you defeated our captain."

"And what of that boy who fought me?" Big Jones growled.

"He walked the plank," Lily said nonchalantly.

Seakane's eyes widened. "No!"

Jones was clearly enjoying every moment of this. "Come on, girl, let us catapult your captain into oblivion."

Lily smiled evilly and stepped up to the big pirate. "Let me do the honours."

"Alright," he said and stepped aside.

But instead of pulling the lever, she drew her cutlass. "Say goodbye," she said, throwing it at Big Jones and hitting him with the flat edge, knocking him out.

A cheer came over the crowd, and they freed Captain Seakane.

"You actually fooled me, ya children" Captain Seakane said, wiping his brow. "Ya little scallywags. Blimming fooled me."

A few hours later the crew had safely returned to the *Harbinger of Death*, taking Big Jones, tied up to the catapult, along with them. The villainous pirate groggily woke up from his unconsciousness.

"Goodbye!" said Captain Seakane.

With that, he, Tom and Lily pulled the lever towards the sky, launching Big Jones and leaving a small smoke trail in their wake.

The *Harbinger of Death* sailed forwards into the blue sea. Tom was leaning on the side rails, and Lily joined him. Both stared out to the sea in silence.

"Well," Tom said finally after what felt like a long silence, "that was a good adventure."

"It was", Lily replied.

"So, when is the next one?"

"I don't know, but I hope it's good," Lily replied. The two shared a smile and stood in silence for the rest of the journey as the sun set below the water.

After several weeks of smooth sailing, they returned to give the treasure to Pirate King Grrrhooley.

P5B

17

THE UNTHINKABLE VOYAGE OF THE UNSINKABLE

P5B

One moonlit, windy night in a distant part of Scotland, *The Unsinkable's* crew were drinking in their local old tavern. The first mate, Andrew Blackbeard, was on a sugar high from drinking too much orange juice. He had a weak spot for orange juice, so the fact that he was already on his 500th glass was not a surprise. Blackbeard was talking animatedly to himself while everybody else was singing sea shanties. Olive, the captain's pet frog, was becoming merry from drinking an entire glass of orange juice and began to join in by creating her own froggy shanty.

To everyone's annoyance, Second Mate Joey Joe began to sing, "Bananas are pink, apples are blue, I wish I could sing with you too!" Joey Joe loved singing, although she was impressively bad at it.

Luckily for the crew, Olive, the frog mascot, told her off. "You imbecile, will you shut it?"

Joey stopped, embarrassed by her singing mistakes. Suddenly the lights went out, and with a large stomping sound, Pirate King Grrrhooley entered.

Banging his fists down on the table, he declared, "Me

hearties! Will you stop with your singing and screeching and listen up!"

Joey Joe rolled her eyes in disgust, annoyed that he'd broken the merry atmosphere.

Speaking to Captain One-Eyed Skink, he continued, "I need your crew to go on a dangerous adventure for me. I need you to travel to an island, San Andrés, just off the coast of Colombia. There you should find a treasure. This treasure will form a missing piece of a 21-piece puzzle. When all the silver, gold and jewels are assembled, something magical will happen!"

Grrrhooley trailed off into silence. The captain of *The Unsinkable*, One-Eyed Skink, asked in concern, "Are you okay, Pirate King?"

"I'm fine," he replied. "I'm just imagining all of the treasure," he continued with a mesmerised look on his face.

Joey Joe rolled her eyes again, not appreciating being told what to do. Captain One-Eyed Skink stepped in to speak to her crew. "My marvellous, majestic crew. Think of all the treasure! Let's gather our things and create our plan." She paused to get their attention. "Shall we do it, me mateys?"

With a resounding sound, they shouted, "Aye aye, Captain!"

After their mission briefing from Grrrhooley, the crew got ready to set sail. They headed back to Bruntsfield Bay to *The Unsinkable* to start their voyage, but little do they know, Briny Beard, their mortal enemy, would be close on their tail.

The Unsinkable and its crew were sailing peacefully by the sandy beaches of the west coast of Ireland and towards the Cliff of Moher. Luckily, it was a stormy day, as *The Unsinkable* was an ironic ship in that it coped well in stormy seas but struggled on calm waters.

The captain asked Blackbeard, "Where did you put the shovels?"

Andrew looked confused and replied, "I thought you had asked me to pack bubbles, not shovels!"

Olive screamed in frustration to the crew, "He ain't got no shovels, he brought bubbles!"

Joey Joe rolled her eyes, knowing that shovels are the most vital tool when it comes to treasure hunting.

The captain replied, disappointed, "That's a big problem. What are we going to do?"

Olive responded helpfully, "There must be a B&Q here in Ireland. Let's stop here and pick one up."

Once they had docked *The Unsinkable* at the harbour, they headed towards B&Q. The crew were walking cautiously, as they grew up hearing of old mythical stories about the Irish Banshees who roamed the land and how they were not massive fans of pirate crews.

On the other side of the Island of Ireland, a group of Banshees sensed the arrival of these strangers to their island and set off on a search.

As they neared the car park of B&Q, a cold wind blew over the crew. Olive and Captain shared a frightened glance.

"Do you sense that someone is watching us?" gulped Olive.

Suddenly the crew were deafened by a high-pitched screeching sound. Turning around, they spotted a group of ghostly figures which had long, translucent white hair, pale skin and looked like they had just been resurrected from a long sleep. As if they were floating towards them, the Banshees, wearing ripped gowns, outstretched their long bony fingers and opened their mouths to wail and scare the pirates away. "Ahhh."

The crew winced in pain, falling to the ground with the sheer noise of their wailing.

Joey Joe started to remember a myth she was told of how when Banshees experienced singing, it caused them to flee.

"I've got this" she declared to the crew.

Trembling and with knees knocking, Joey Joe walked towards the Banshees, attempting to look them eye to eye but began to feel less confident in her singing ability. In fright, she started singing even worse than usual. Her pirate-mates knew to cover their ears to block out her terrible tune. "ThErE oNcE wAs a sHip ThAt WeNt To SeA. pLeAsE gO aWaY, YOU SILLY BANSHEES!"

The Irish Banshees heard her awful, shrieking voice, and unexpectantly they stopped and stepped back in shock at her terrible tones. Joey's singing caused so much pain to their ears that they collapsed to the ground, completely knocked out cold in B&Q's carpark.

"Joey Joe, that was one of your worst songs we've ever heard you sing. It was so beautiful, thank you!" exclaimed Olive.

With their new shovels in hand, *The Unsinkable* crew celebrated Joey Joe's success by throwing a party for their next leg of the voyage, Cuba.

In his mission briefing, Grrrhooley had given the crew clear instructions to stop in Cuba and meet with an old sage who would give them the exact directions to the treasure. After five days sailing over the stormy north Atlantic Ocean, they finally arrived in Cuba. The crew tied up their ship and got ready to disembark.

"What's a sage again?" asked Andrew, confused with the task at hand.

"A sage is like a fortune teller, I think," replied Olive.

The crew made their way along an old, cracked road, leading to the sage's house which looked more like an old, small wooden hut with a drab and plain exterior. Captain One-Eyed Skink bravely knocked on the door and took a step backwards as the door creaked open. Inside, the hut was pitch black and it looked like it hadn't been visited in decades. Standing by the door was an old man with a long beard, paper-white hair, multiple wrinkles, and wearing a red velvet robe and a purple turban with a feather on top.

"We're looking for directions to treasure in San Andrés. Pirate King Grrrhooley has sent us," explained the captain.

Clutching his golden walking stick, the old sage whispered in his old croaky voice, "First, sail to Colombia and find the island San Andrés. There you will find the underwater cave where you will dive to find your treasure." The sage then handed them a treasure map which would guide them to the exact point.

"X marks the spot," grinned Olive.

They turned and smiled to each other, delighted that everything was going to plan. When they left the sage, beaming with happiness, they decided to stop at a local shop to purchase some Cuban cigars.

"Let's go!" cried Joey Joe.

"No! Not for you! You're too young to smoke!" said the captain.

"Yeah," replied Olive.

"You can't either! Silly frog!" the captain snapped.

After their purchases, the crew turned a corner on the street. The happiness of the moment quickly dissipated when they spotted a familiar figure... It was Briny Beard, their mortal enemy, smoking a gravy-flavoured cigar. The scurvy sea dog was unmistakable with his huge bushy orange beard, loose trousers and his wooden peg leg. He was the most bloodthirsty pirate on the seven seas and was always looking for more treasure. He was obviously here after the treasure the crew were looking for.

Briny Beard swiftly turned towards them and aimed his enormous super stinky gravy cannon straight at the captain. With a cunning smile, Briny rushed towards the pirates.

"RUN!" yelled Olive.

"Ahhhh!" they screamed as they ran as fast as they could while Briny Beard was furiously shooting his canon at them.

Splat!

Briny got his first victim as he covered the captain with his super stinky gravy.

"Noooooo!" wailed the captain as she shuddered in fear at the taste and smell of the gravy. She had a severe case of gravy-phobia.

Joey Joe began singing in fear, Blackbeard attempted to fight back and Olive led Briny Beard around a corner. Out of pure luck and chance, Briny Beard turned the corner too sharply and his tiny, chubby leg got stuck in-between the cracks of the old road. He couldn't get out.

"I'll get you next time!" shouted Briny Beard as the crew quickly rush to tend to the captain, who was howling like a wolf due to her gravy agony. Spluttering and coughing, the captain was almost hyperventilating. Her gravy-phobia was really kicking in.

"It's just gravy, Captain!" Olive said reassuringly. Together they lifted the captain and escaped to the port. Safely on board again, all they then needed to do was follow the map and find the treasure to bring it back to Pirate King Grrrhooley. Celebrating with their age-appropriate, frog-friendly, tobacco-free Cuban cigars and OJ beer, *The Unsinkable* crew continued their journey to find the treasure.

After escaping Briny Beard, the crew were so distracted in their celebrations that they didn't notice the danger of the calm seas ahead. All was not well. Remember, *The Unsinkable* was an ironic ship and sailed well on stormy seas but badly on calm seas.

"We've got a problem," said Olive.

"What is it?" replied One-Eyed Skink.

"It's calm waters..." Olive's voice faded into silence.

It was becoming clear that *The Unsinkable* couldn't cope in the calm waters. It was zigzagging. It was flipping. It was dancing on the water. In fear, the captain cried, "We need to think of a plan quickly!"

Then disaster struck. *The Unsinkable* did the unthinkable and started to sink!

Blackbeard suddenly remembered a scene from *The Titanic*. "We need to throw our doors and belongings off the boat, like *The Titanic!*" he yelled. Surprisingly, the whole crew agreed, desperate to look after their precious ship. So, in a panic, they started to pull off doors and throw them overboard along with their items.

"Nothing's happening!" shrieked Joey Joe.

"It's not working!" the captain declared.

"What should we do?" asked Olive.

The crew rattled their brains, trying to think of solutions.

"We need to think of the nature of this ship... It does the opposite of what it should do," mulled Olive.

"Well, if it does the opposite, the opposite of floating is sinking. What would make it sink?" asked Blackbeard.

"Holes!" shouted the captain.

"Holes?" Joey Joe said confused.

"Yes! Epic idea, Captain!" exclaimed Olive, realising that what the captain said was true. "Let's poke holes in the boat, that should cause it to float rather than sink," suggested Olive.

"Well, there are no other plans, we might as well try it," said Joey Joe hopefully.

In a hurry, the crew grabbed their swords and shovels and started making holes. Amazingly, it started to work! After a few moments, they felt themselves rising with the boat. The vessel started to stay afloat.

"It works! It works!" celebrated the crew.

"This is stupendously incredible!" cried Olive.

"It's unbelievable! We have saved the ship!" Joey Joe exclaimed, relieved.

"Hang on, we don't have any doors now!" Blackbeard blurted.

"Who cares about doors?!" replied One-Eyed Skink.

"Doors, doors, doors, how I miss the old doors" sung Joey Joe.

"Ughhh, not again!" sighed the crew.

After their struggles to keep *The Unsinkable* together, the crew headed towards San Andrés. The rest of the journey was smooth sailing. As the sun went down, the crew readied themselves for the new day ahead of them and the treasure they would hopefully find. At last, they were nearly there!

Once they arrived in the area near the underwater cave, the crew grabbed their shovels and squeezed into their snorkelling gear. Now they were ready to dive into the ocean to hunt for the treasure. Due to the crew being so elated from getting to this point in the journey, they forgot that Olive was very bad at navigation and gave her the duty of following the map and leading them to the spot where the treasure was buried.

Olive announced, "To the treasure!"

Olive led them south instead of north and right instead of left. They were heading in the wrong direction, towards the dark side of the ocean! In the depths of the sea, oblivious to Olive's bad sense of direction, Blackbeard noticed a dark shadow swimming towards them.

"Does anybody else see that shadow coming this way?" trembled Joey Joe.

Frozen in fear, the crew started to realise there was not one but several creatures heading in their direction. Deadly predators. The largest shark ever discovered, *Otodus megalodon*, was on their tail along with a wild breed of sea dragons and the colossal squid, kraken. The sea dragon had green scaley skin and jewels encrusted in its horns, and their claws were sharper than a sabretooth's mouth. The huge squid had long tentacles, and its skin was slimy and navy blue.

"That's some cracker of a kraken!" yelped Blackbeard.

"Run! I mean, SWIM!" screamed Olive as they all turned in the opposite direction as fast as they can. The megalodon sped at them with its silvery-grey eyes glistening with hunger. The kraken was not far behind, with the killer eyes of the sea dragon piercing the crew with fear.

"We're going to die, we are going to die, we are going to die!" Joey Joe sang repeatedly.

Joey Joe was panicking and struggling to swim, so Andrew Blackbeard tried to help by catching an innocent fish and launching it towards the megalodon. They heard a small cry out of the fish as it stalled the shark for a moment, but the sea dragon started to speed up and seemed to be travelling as fast as lightning.

Olive thought it was all over until a tiny glowing light appeared in the distance, causing everything to be still. As the light got closer, a faint sound of music started to get louder. It was the sound of smooth jazz. The crew could not believe what they were hearing or seeing. Famous sea celebrity SpongeBob SquarePants was heading in their direction with Patrick Star and Gary the snail following closely behind. Patrick was playing smooth jazz on the saxophone which was causing the monstrous sea creatures to stay calm and still.

"Don't you dare hurt them!" SpongeBob declared with authority.

The monstrous creatures soon backed off and drifted back to their home in the dark side of the ocean. The crew were so pleased, they rushed to greet and thank their saviours.

"SpongeBob! Wow! I can't believe it's really you," said Captain One-Eyed Skink.

"I watch you on TV!" added in Blackbeard.

"What's TV?" wondered Patrick.

"Happy to help! It's always nice to meet some fans," replied SpongeBob confidently.

"Meow," mumbled Gary (who didn't have a huge vocabulary).

SpongeBob SquarePants handed a golden key to Olive.

"What's this for?" she asked.

"Don't you know? It's obviously the key for the treasure! You will need this to help you," he replied.

"Pirate King Grrrhooley has been in touch and we've been waiting for you guys," chipped in Patrick.

As SpongeBob, Patrick and Gary swam off, the crew realised from looking at the sage's treasure map, that the chase had in fact led them back onto the right path and that they were only around the corner from the underwater cave. Joey Joe spotted the treasure poking out of the sand and with the help of Andrew Blackbeard and their shovels from B&Q, they retrieved the treasure and heaved it back out of the water.

Once all on board, Captain One-Eyed Skink told the crew, "I think it's time to go home."

"I can't wait to get back and see Grrrhooley's reaction to the treasure," said Andrew Blackbeard.

Olive chipped in, "I'll lead the ship home. After all, practice makes perfect!"

So, they set off home with Olive leading the way and the captain keeping a very close eye on her. Exhausted yet exhilarated from their victorious adventures, *The Unsinkable* crew drifted off into the sunset singing, "Who lives in a pineapple under the sea? SpongeBob SquarePants!" And they returned with the treasure, giving it to Pirate King Grrrhooley.

P2A

18

THE SNAIL AND THE PIZZA
P2A

It was another day at Bruntsfield Pirate School and pirate class 2A were arriving at Pirate Bay. Pirate Class 2A boarded their ship—the *Arthur's Sail*. The huge boat had seen many wars and had been attacked countless times. Even though the seas were rough, *Arthur's Sail* was incredibly sturdy, and, some could argue, an unbeatable force. Over the years, there were many repairs made to its surface, but this added to its pirate charm. Mounted on the hull of the ship were some solid gold canons, and in the sky flew red raggy sails with a skull and crossbones scowling in the middle. A crow's nest sat on the tallest mast made from an old barrel acting as a watch tower.

Once aboard the boat, pirate class 2A grabbed daggers, cutlasses and machetes. Their first lesson of the day was sword fighting.

Captian Whitehook was watching through her left eye, as the right was covered by an eyepatch. She was inspecting the pirates' techniques from afar. Her hair was long, curly and brown, and a large black hat was perched on her head. She wore an abundance of jewellery. Thick gold necklaces hung around her neck. Being a captain was tiring, and in her old age her patience was wearing thin. If any pirate pupils were caught talking, they'd be forced to walk the plank.

Captain Whitehook's accomplice was Greeny, a magical teddy who had sailed the seven seas. Greeny was known for eating chocolate cake, apples and giving everyone cuddles. The teddy despised being wet, which was unfortunate as this was something which was quite common when living on a boat!

The pirate class were ducking and diving, continuing to sword fight with their talk partners, when suddenly, there was a loud noise heard on the ship.

The head honcho had arrived blowing a horn.

It was Pirate King Grrrhooley who had gained the attention of everyone. He had a special mission for pirate class 2A. Pirate King Grrrhooley rolled out an old, dishevelled map which had a large X marked on a country. This country was shaped like a boot, and when looking closer, the pirates read "ITALY" in big capital letters. He explained to the class that there was some treasure to be found.

He shouted, "Are you ready to find some treasure?"

The pirate pupils chanted "Aye, Aye, Captain."

Arthur's Sail's first mate was called Capt'n Capt'n Capt'n. As Captain Whitehook's right hand, Capt'n Capt'n Capt'n was in charge when no other captains were around. She spent most of her days eating sardines and daydreaming on the hull of the boat. Third in command was Sailor Master Cheeky. He was given this name due to his cheeky charm. He was usually smiling, although his worst nightmare was creepy crawlies. If he spotted one, he would let out a very loud scream and jump up into Capt'n Capt'n Capt'n's arms.

The team of pirates prepared for their journey and set sail, aiming to reach the Mediterranean Sea. On their way, they passed the Strait of Gibraltar, where the waves were growing choppy and a storm was brewing nearby.

All of a sudden, a two-headed hairy monster came bellowing from the sea. It was Tarya, a viscous being who was rumoured to swallow people up in a single gulp. Poor Tommy, a trainee pirate, got knocked off the boat and was chomped up, turning the monster into Tomtarya. It appeared to have a new head which was growing on its side, and it got stronger. It was hearsay that this monster had only one weakness. This weakness was cuddles. Hearing this from previous journeys, Greeny jumped to the rescue and landed on Tomtarya. He gave the monster his fluffy, cuddly bear cuddles which caused the monster to melt away. The sea monster shrunk down and down to the size of an ant, and Captain Whitehook flipped it in the air and flicked it away.

It was a close call, but *Arthur's Sail* continued its journey to reach its destination—Italy! The pirate ship docked, and the crew disembarked. The sun was shining and pirate class 2A could smell pizzas, and people were drinking coffee and eating ice cream. The X on the map led the pirates all the way to Rome to the Colosseum where the special pirate treasure was buried underneath.

Captain Whitehook looked amazed at the amphitheatre and took it upon herself to guide pirate class 2A inside. When searching through the ruins, out of nowhere her archnemesis, Captain Squishy Nose, appeared. Captain Squishy Nose was a nasty fellow who was a master pickpocket. His favourite hobby was to creep up on anyone who happened to have treasure. He had a massive sticky nose, shaped like a pickle. He fired one nose shot, hurling sticky snot and catching Captain Whitehook, who was trapped to the wall in the icky goo.

Up stood Capt'n Capt'n Capt'n, who had a thought up a cunning plan. Sailor Master Cheeky was going to distract Captain Squishy Nose by using his cheeky charm. He quickly thought up a cheeky dance and began to sing "Baby Shark". This mesmerized Captain Squishy Nose, causing stars to float around his head. Meanwhile, Capt'n Capt'n Capt'n was using her many sardine cans she'd gathered to build an enormous cage. This cage was so solid that nobody could break out. Sailor Master Cheeky began to tickle Captain Squishy Nose's nose, causing him to trip backwards, hurtling into the cage.

Captain Squishy Nose was defeated. All of Pirate class 2A cheered, "Hooray for Capt'n Capt'n Capt'n and Sailor Master Cheeky!"

Pirate class 2A continued hunting for the hidden treasure. They searched and searched but couldn't find a thing. There was not even a clue to guide them to their destination.

Then, out of nowhere appeared a diamond encrusted snail. It was glistening in the sun, and it began to speak in a small, tiny voice. He seemed very distressed. The diamond snail squeaked, "Captain Squishy Nose attacked us! He stole my family and wanted to harvest our shells which are made from precious jewels!"

Capt'n Capt'n Capt'n knelt down to the little snail's level. "We've captured the horrible man! Let's unite the snail with his family!"

Once the snails were united, the diamond snail offered to guide pirate class 2A to the hidden treasure. Diamond snails have a very special power! The magical creatures can sense jewels and gold through a magnetic force. After several hours of moving at a snail's pace, they found a secret passageway. They went down some stairs which led to a gigantic pizza oven. To reach the treasure, the diamond snail revealed that the pirates were to cook a special pizza. This pizza was to be cooked to perfection, not one second overcooked and not one second undercooked. Otherwise, the oven would explode and the treasure would disappear.

In the pizza pan, the pirates mixed up a unique combination of toppings based on their pirate adventures. They sprinkled some sweet pineapple, juicy mozzarella and stinky sardines on the dough. The oven door opened, and the pirates carefully placed the pizza in to cook, keeping an eye on the crust to make sure it was crisp and golden.

When it looked ready, they took it out of the oven and used a pizza cutter to chop it into slices. The diamond snail took a bite, shouting "BUONISSIMA!" They had passed the test!

The ground opened and the treasure was revealed. But what was it? There was a golden pizza box. They had been given struct instructions by Pirate King Grrrhooley not to open it, so instead they headed back to their ship and began their very long journey back to Bruntsfield Pirate School, based at Pirate Bay. When they arrived, they gave the box to Pirate King Grrrhooley, eager to know what was inside.

P6B

19

KINDNESS CONQUERS ALL!

P6B

It was a delightful summery day by the Scottish coastline. Actually, no! This is Scotland we're talking about; the wind was howling, and the clouds looked like they were about to burst. These children didn't mind though, as they were used to this weather.

Today was the day that they were going to Italy to study pasta. Everyone was so excited for this splendid voyage. But little did P6B know that there would be a slight change in plans. They set to work on doing their jobs for the day. Kahu and Jess were busy gathering sticks for the fire that Isla, Ruth and Sam were making. Martha and Jad's height was coming in handy reaching for the tall willow branches. Meanwhile Alice, Esmé, Levi, Maia and Zita were returning from a successful fishing trip. Anna and Lennon gasped as they heaved out some impressive fish. Izzy, Jude, Hank, Callum and Breagha were collecting rooibos leaves while Ahmad, Samuel and Paul were learning how to make them into tea. Chandler and Levi were taking photos of different plants with their iPads, while Charlie and Nubia were identifying the trees. Tanisha, Aidan, Sedef, Cora and Moses were practising their map-reading skills. David and

Vaani were sitting on a dry patch of sand by the trees with nothing to do but chill.

Suddenly loud footsteps crunched on the sand. The children looked around and saw Mr. Gilhooley. He had big news.

"There's been a change in plans, no more spaghetti silliness or conchiglie craze in Italy. I'm sending you on a special journey. A journey to find treasure!"

The whole class whooped and cheered; this was every child's dream, almost like a pirate adventure. There was whispering and then someone shouted out, "You should be called Pirate King Grrrhooley!"

Another voice said, "And Mrs Foley should be called Captain O' Foley!"

Mrs Foley then suggested she could be called Captain Peg Leg in case her knee got worse. The class giggled and agreed. Mrs Foley then rummaged in her bag and found a pirate hat to wear. The children cheered again.

Pirate King Grrrhooley handed Captain Peg Leg a battered old map, and this was the start of a fantastic journey.

A journey to deepest Darkest Peru...

In preparation for the voyage, Ben MacBear and his little friend Ted had been in the kitchen making sweets for the teachers, but there was a problem. Ben and Ted had mixed up the salt and sugar (an easy mistake to make, especially for bears). Ben and Ted were so excited by the news of their new and most excellent adventure that they forgot to taste the sweets before giving them to Captain Peg Leg, Miss Lai and Mrs Pallucci.

Naturally, the adults thought that the sweets would be yummy, so they took a handful and stuffed it into their mouths. But of course they were too salty, and the adults passed out!

Ben, Ted and the children ran to fetch buckets of water, and on Ben's command the children threw the water at the adults to bring them round. They got soaked. Feeling sorry for themselves, the adults decided to take themselves into a corner of the ship to rest and gain their strength back.

Lying on the deck, Ben saw Captain Peg Leg's hat. It had shrunk in the water. Ben took the hat and it fitted perfectly.

"The very thing!"

Mrs Foley smiled approvingly, and said, "Well, if the hat fits..."

All the children shouted three cheers for their new captain —Captain Ben MacBear. He looked quite splendid in his black pirate's hat, the red ribbons going well with the red of his wee kilt. The perfect captain for their pirate adventure. The children then heard a gentle cough and looked down to see Ted. He looked at them hopefully.

"Three cheers for First Mate Ted!"

"No!" cried Ben, and the children gasped in surprise.

Then Ben smiled and said, "He's my bestie, so it's three cheers for Best Mate Ted!"

Before long, Captain Ben and Best Mate Ted stood at the helm of the ship, directing their new crew of eager young pirate sailors. It was now all calm after the commotion of the sweetie disaster. The children were scrubbing and polishing the decks. When everything was all clean and shipshape, school uniforms were cut and adapted to make their pirate outfits. Neckerchiefs and headscarves completed the look. Keen to show off their outfits, the children started to dance their sea shanties and began to sing, "Sailing, we are sailing..."

All that ceilidh dancing came in handy, as the children were twirling and twirling around the boat.

After a long time, a faint outline of an island came into view. First, they anchored the ship in the bay and went ashore. On the island they used their weaving skills to weave baskets to pick some oranges. Soon, the baskets were full, and they decided to go look for some sugar cane.

After everyone boarded the ship, they were back on track

for Darkest Peru. Everybody settled down again and they continued their voyage to "The Home for Retired Bears." Time passed quickly, as the children looked after the ship and followed the instructions from their new captain and best mate.

At last, new land came into view. It was Darkest Peru. Their journey was almost complete. Excited by the thought of the treasure, the children made for land. Some, too impatient to wait to be rowed ashore, jumped in and began to swim. Luckily, swimming lessons are given at Bruntsfield Primary. All made it ashore safely.

And now for the treasure.

After everyone was off the ship, all the crew were very keen to find the treasure. An enthusiasm which unfortunately resulted in chaos. All doing anything they could, climbing up trees, looking in bushes, lifting rocks and even looking for X marks the spot. Until someone found two sticks crossed over in an X shape. Everyone rushed over to help their crewmate dig. They dug and dug but couldn't find anything.

Best Mate Ted came over and explained they could use their map-reading skills to find the Home for Retired Bears. And off they went, a happy crew of pirates led by two bears.

When, eventually, Captain Ben MacBear and Best Mate Ted strode through the doors of the Home for Retired Bears, they noticed an old lady bear sitting at a dark table at the back of the room. She seemed to be playing cards but stood up with a soft groan to welcome them in. Then the old lady bear smiled and laughed, took off her spectacles and offered her paw.

Captain Ben MacBear quickly introduced himself and explained that he was here to collect the box of treasure. The old bear said that she would help them, but first the children needed to help with some chores for all of bears in the home. Captain Ben smiled politely and said that of course they would. Being kind to your elders was a very important thing.

The children were put into groups and given their tasks.

The first group got straight to work to help. They rushed into the kitchen to make tea, but the kettle was broken. They also noticed that the toaster was broken too and passed on the information to Captain Ben. After a bit of thinking, they realised they could use their fire building skills to build a fire to boil the water and to toast the bread.

The next group went to the ship to fetch the fresh oranges that they picked earlier on the island. They also grabbed the sugar, after checking it really was the sugar this time, and rushed back to the home to make the marmalade for the bears. The basket weaving group realised that they could shape some twigs and sticks to make toasting forks. When the children had finished their tasks, they gathered in the garden outside the Home for Retired Bears. And waited.

There was one group missing. It was the group collecting the bread from the kitchen for the toasted marmalade sandwiches. Ted was with them, and he was helping the children find the bread box. Cupboards were opened, drawers were pulled and Ted inspected, but still no bread box. Finally, they spotted something in the darkest corner, of the darkest cupboard, in the Home for Retired Bears in Darkest Peru.

It was the bread box.

It was a huge box, which took the efforts of all the children to drag into the middle of the kitchen floor. Opening it, they found several loaves of freshly made bead, but there was something else under a neatly folded tea towel. Ted jumped to attention and directed the children to it. It was the Box of Treasure!

Cheers filled the air, and the children lifted the box in the air (taking care not to open it), with Ted standing proudly on the lid, and made their way to the garden.

"We found it! We found the treasure box!"

"Three cheers for us! Three cheers for the Home for Retired Bears."

"And three cheers for kindness," said the old bear gently. "It was your kindness in helping us old bears that led you to the treasure."

The celebrations that followed would not be forgotten. A most splendid end to the quest for treasure. As the last rays of sunshine dipped away, Captain Ben reminded them that they needed to get back to the ship, back to the teachers and back to school. The children all lined up, in register order of course, and awaited their orders. Best Mate Ted led the way, still on top of the Box of Treasure, and the children followed. Captain Ben stood at the rear nodding happily to himself. Then he leaned towards the old bear and said with a smile, "Your nephew sends you lots of love."

As the proud crew of P6B walked the long track to their mighty ship, they noticed the weather had changed, a wind was blowing, and the raging waves looked as if they were hungry for fish and ships! It would be far too dangerous to set sail in this. The crew had no idea how to get home, but Captain Ben knew what to do.

"I have the very thing!" he said and rummaged in his sporran and brought out a huge tube of glue.

He then asked the children who had been practising basket weaving to help make huge wings. All the pieces of willow that they had collected earlier would be useful now. Captain Ben got the glue and handed it to Best Mate Ted. *Always safer for an older bear to do the gluing*, he thought. In no time at all, Ted had hopped, skipped and jumped around the ship, carefully applying glue as the children held the wings in place. Soon the job was done.

Once more, Captain Ben rummaged in his sporran and brought out a pawful of wires and connectors. He then signalled to Best Mate Ted. And once more Ted hopped, skipped and jumped, this time around the children and into their rucksacks. IPads were tossed to Ben, who then proceeded to hook up each of them, to create a massive power source for the mighty ship and so they could use satellite navigation. When they finished building their fantastic flying ship, everyone climbed aboard and waited for one enormous wave to launch their flight.

The mighty flying ship started to climb up into the starry night sky. It flew in circles around the Home for Retired Bears, everyone shouting their goodbyes until they were at a good height to fly home. The old bear had given all of them piles of delicious marmalade sandwiches for their hard work and journey home. Everyone was content with their sandwiches made with perfection and love.

They flew home, munching on marmalade sandwiches and sharing experiences of this most amazing adventure. By now, Mrs Foley, Mrs Pallucci and Miss Lai had fully recovered and listened in astonishment to the children's most extraordinary tale. The journey passed quickly as stories were told and retold, each time growing with wonder!

As they approached Edinburgh, the children looked once again at the maps for a safe place to land their mighty flying ship. The familiar rooftops of Bruntsfield came into view, and with Captain Ben at the helm and Best Mate Ted calling out instructions, they carefully landed on the roof of Bruntsfield Primary School. Making use of the final pieces of willow and the extra pieces of rope that they had made with plant leaves, they jumped down the sides of the flying boat, down the sides of the school building and onto the playground.

Puzzled by the noise, Mr. Gilhooley came down from his office and outside to the playground. Captain Ben saluted their Pirate King and signalled for the children to bring forward their Box of Treasure, with Best Mate Ted still standing on the lid.

Mrs. Foley then stepped forward holding a plate.

"Perhaps you would like the final marmalade sandwich while you hear of our most excellent adventure."

P3B

20

TRIP TO BANGLADESH

P3B

Waves were rolling into pretty Pirate Bay. It was a beautiful day and all was calm until Pirate King Grrrhooley burst into the bay. He was riding his bike, out of breath and looking rather suspicious. He interrupted P3B, who were quietly working on their navigation project. "I need your help, P3B and *Lazer* ship! You have to find the mysterious, secret treasure and bring it back to the bay. If you return it, something magical will happen!"

In amazement, many of the children dropped their maths into the water. It all got soggy and impossible to read. "Oh nooooooo!" cried Scarlett and Nefeli.

Pirate King Grrrhooley helped Adelise and Mehnoor fish it out and then continued. "It is going to be terribly risky and it is only fifty-fifty whether you will be successful. Do you accept the challenge?"

Ilyana and Adair were excited but wanted to finish their maths first. Everyone else was super keen, so once they had finished, they listened more about where it was hidden.

"You must navigate your way to Bangladesh and locate the treasure! Here is a map."

They studied the map closely, and after an excited discussion, they all agreed it was a fantastic idea. They quickly got ready to go. William and Orfeas started fixing the ship, as it had run out of power on its last mission to Africa. Advik wrote a letter to his parents saying how he would miss them. Finlay, Cora and Alfie helped gather some supplies such as meat, vegetables, Prime and Coca Cola. The P3B team then set sail and went on the exciting, yet risky, around-the-world adventure.

After a few hours, they came across a gigantic, underwater volcano where there were lava bombs and lots of rocks to navigate through. In fear, Chloe made a mysterious, growling and gurgling sound. "Arghrrrrrrrrrrrr." This made Martin jump, knocking his glasses into the water. Quick as a flash, Manuella dived in, collecting them before they sank any deeper!

Aiman was sitting at the bow of the boat navigating. By now, he really needed to go to the toilet but hated going. He crossed his legs so tightly but was holding for just too long. Cindy demanded Aiman go to the toilet. He sprinted as fast as he could, went in and shut the door. While he was in there, the ship suddenly jerked and a spanner from the ship's toolbox flung into the air and wedged itself in the door. "Oopsie!" the crew said. This unfortunately blocked the door, and now Aiman was stuck in the toilet!

Cindy realised there was now no one that wanted to navigate the ship, so she decided to stay and guide the ship through the unexpected obstacles herself, leaving Aiman to find his way out.

Next, the brave pirates of P3B had to navigate through Evil Pirate Bay where Chicken Pox Baddy was sitting on an ice castle. Apparently, the cold ice helped with the itchiness of his chicken pox. Unfortunately, the *Lazer* had been given the wrong information which had sent them to this dangerous area.

Chicken Pox Baddy spotted the *Lazer* and P3B sneakily

trying to pass. He rubbed his nose against the ice in disgust! "We muffffft thstop Pee thwee." Determined to stop them, he swung off the block of ice.

Captain Killian started a sword fight with him but unfortunately caught chicken pox from Chicken Pox Baddy. She defeated the baddy, who then cried like a baby really loudly. "Boooooo hoooooo!"

Killian went to get chicken pox cream from the toilet to help. Killian remembered that the door was stuck and heard Aiman shouting from inside. "Mwwwaaahhh!" Killian managed to creep under the toilet door to Aiman.

Suddenly, the ship jerked again, forcing maths shapes to be catapulted under the door, blocking the way under. Fortunately, Killian was amazing at climbing, so managed to climb over with the cream and Aiman on her back. Cindy caught her as she jumped down. The cream worked successfully, and now Killian was free of the pox and ready to go again!

By now, everyone was getting rather hungry, as they had finished all their food supplies. Chester had an idea to fish from the side of the ship to catch something for their tea. Luckily, Julek had brought his special water filter so they could drink the water from the sea. They then heard a very happy yelp of delight from the end of the ship. Everyone looked around to see what it was.

The team realised Tawheed and Alexian had caught the biggest fish they had ever seen! It was humungous! Astrid and Harrison then had an idea to get another drink. They had been busy making a special machine that fired at the passing palm trees, knocking coconuts off down a chute and into a basket. The coconuts then went down the chute back to the *Lazer* for everyone to share the milk. Yum!

With their bellies full, the team continued their mission. Looking at the map, it showed that the special treasure was hidden in a food market in Bangladesh. They convinced

Captain Killian to go into the food market on bikes, as this would be fast. They had heard that the food market was haunted, so they wanted to be as quick as possible.

Suddenly, Captain Killian got a fright and jumped. She swerved on her bike and fell, breaking her arm. "Ouch!!! That hurts so much!" she screamed.

While everyone was checking that Killian was OK, a magical dog crept up to Cindy and started whispering to her in English. "The key to the cellar where the treasure is, is hidden in a watermelon. You need to take the key and unlock the brightly coloured cellar door. You will then find a statue of a golden monkey. The treasure is behind it."

With the new information, the team cycled back through the food market and searched through all the watermelons. "I've found it!" whispered Leila. Leila passed it secretly to Chloe, who then took the key and found the brightly coloured door. Cautiously, Killian turned the key (with her other arm) and opened the door.

Inside, the golden monkey statue stood in front of a glistening treasure box. However, it was guarded by a pack of wild Markos and Nicholases, who began chasing them. Abhi and Theo distracted them with empty bottles of Prime and Coca Cola. Cindy got out her lightsabre, *vmmm vmmm*, and scared them all away.

P3B grabbed the treasure box, cycled quickly back to the ship and set sail back to Bruntsfield Pirate Bay.

A few weeks later, the treasure box finally made it back to Bruntsfield to Pirate King Grrrhooley. Lucille and Safa brought the box to Pirate King Grrrhooley.

"Thank you so much! As your reward there are some extra maths sheets for you to do as homework!" the king said.

They all cheered, especially Auke, as he loved extra maths.

P7B

21

BOBERIÑO II AND THE LOST TREASURE OF MICRONESIA

P7B

It was a warm mid-afternoon as Pirate King Grrrhooley and his pirate crew were sitting on the deck of their ship, *Boberiño II*. Life had been fairly boring of late, but the crew were grateful of the peace and tranquillity as they came to terms with the wreckage of their previous vessel, *Boberiño I*.

The crew had been entertained by Pirate King Grrrhooley's stories of treasure, battle and sunken ships. Grrrhooley was proud of his fleet of twenty-one glorious ships and prouder of his ships' captains, who had become more like a family to him than just sea-faring friends.

Captain Knails Knusty was in charge of *Boberiño II* and was revered for travelling the Pacific Ocean in the most stylish ship known to man or woman. When Knails Knusty was just seven years old she fought off a group of giant crabs but unfortunately lost one of her eyes. In the battle, her hands and nails were damaged, which in turn sparked her love for fake nails and stylish eye patches. Knusty had two tattoos on her left thigh and a blue bandana. Captain Knails Knusty had travelled to hundreds of countries including an unknown island where she found her latest partner in crime, Capy Capy, a capybara.

The two main talispeople of Knusty's crew were First Mate Froggo and Pirate Pearl. First Mate Froggo had been with Knusty's crew for a while and hoped soon to have another adventure like they'd had in the old days. First Mate Froggo had joined the crew when he was only a little laddie. He'd been lost at sea and had hung onto a giant frog to stop himself from drowning. The great sea had almost swallowed him whole, but the mighty green amphibian had been his saviour and took him to the safety of a giant ship. That ship had been *Boberiño I*. From that point on, Froggo was extremely grateful for the crew, and he swore to always protect them, so he practised the art of the cutlass. Even although there was an incident with some avocados which ended in *Boberiño I* being cut clean in half, the crew all loved him as a brother.

After some time, Froggo decided to grow a pirate goatee and a moustache to show his bravery against those evil avocados and their 'orrid, foul, beast-like skin. To Froggo there was only one creation on Earth which deserved a lumpy bumpy warty outer skin, and that was of course his beloved frogs. First Mate Froggo had a feisty pet frog called Roberto.

Pirate Pearl, however, hadn't been with the crew quite so long and had been no part of the *Boberino I* debacle. She was excited to go treasure hunting with her new crew and wanted to feel the wind in her hair and salt on her lips.

For the time being however, they were quite content just relaxing and playing card games as their mascot, Capy Capy Capybara, ran around entertaining them with death metal anthems and vigorous jigs. Capy Capy Capybara had worked in a circus but escaped and swam away to that secret island where he had been saved by Captain Knails Knusty. Capy Capy Capybara was a tough old rodent, and legend had it that he had once beaten up sixteen police officers just because they made fun of his front teeth!

The crew knew that Pirate King Grrrhooley was about to

make an announcement and that they soon would be anchors away and off on a new adventure. Their only concern was that they would encounter their archnemesis, the legendary Bearded Barry! Bearded Barry was an evil and hugely annoying man! When he was twelve years old, he was at James Gillespie's Bay captaining a rival fleet, and his only friend was a panda named Rubert. The reason Barry hated Bruntsfield so much was because one night when he was sleeping, a sneaky pirate from Bruntsfield Bay stole his panda Rubert! Barry never saw him again. No wonder he was so evil—he was definitely a pirate with a score to settle.

Barry was easily identifiable. A genetic mutation had caused his nose to be detachable and turned into a lasso. Barry often used this to his advantage. Despite Barry being incredibly annoying, he was also extremely smart—not a good combination for his enemies.

Pirate King Grrrhooley summoned all the ships to discuss their next mission—to find a very valuable treasure on the shores of the Federated States of Micronesia. Knusty's crew knew it would be a difficult task, but after much back slapping and uplifting sea shanties, they were ready for the challenge.

Boberiño II sailed effortlessly across the crystal clear, turquoise sea for almost three whole days when disaster struck! As they were sailing along, they noticed something odd in the water. They kept on sailing, pushing the lingering thoughts aside, until...

The sky became an ominous grey and murky colour and the sea reflected the darkness of the sky. Before the crew could say anything, they smelt vinegar! *Dun dun dunnn!* Suddenly, the dark ocean started to turn unpleasantly underneath the boat's solid planks. The boat started to spin faster and faster, and the crew started to panic. They realised that the whirlpool must be made of vinegar as the smell was becoming more overpowering and *Boberiño II* was struggling.

The planks started to get sticky. The crew climbed up the riggings to escape the swirling vinegar below. They were very concerned because they knew that vinegar was bad for *Boberiño II*. Pirate Pearl took control and tried to steer everyone to safety.

They looked up and were surprised to see the silhouette of Bearded Barry's massive nose and heard his unforgettable laugh. Bearded Barry's hot air balloon flew over them as they were going down into the ocean. First Mate Froggo was still scared from what happened to *Boberiño I* and didn't want to lose a second ship.

Fortunately, the crew saw a giant blue whale glide past the boat. First Mate Froggo suddenly had an idea. He thought he could lure the whale into the whirlpool, and because the whale was so big, it could plug the source of the whirlpool.

He told the rest of the crew his idea, and they all jumped into action. They got a giant fish from the cellar and put it on a pole. They waved it around near the bottom of the whirlpool. The whale licked its lips and paddled towards the fish. In doing so, the whale plugged the whirlpool. The crew jumped up and down in joy because their plan had worked! They were safe!

As the crew set off on their course to the Federated State of Micronesia, they chucked the fish to the whale to say thank you.

Oh, for the rest of their voyage to pass uneventfully would have been heaven, but as we all know the course of true seafarers never runs smoothly.

A few weeks later, the crew saw a misty figure of a tall tree on the shore of an upcoming island. Mesmerised by the tree, the crew swam to the shore to study it in greater detail. As the crew approached the unusual tree, they realised it was not any ordinary tree. The tree had a tree house with a big X made from smaller Xs engraved in the birch wood

Captain Knails Knusty ordered everyone to investigate around the tree house. Capy Capy Capybara climbed up the tree beside the unusual treehouse to get a better view of the surroundings. Capy Capy Capybara noticed a panda carrying a long sword made of bamboo approaching Captain Knails Knusty and shouting in panda language. Capy Capy Capybara climbed down the tree as fast as he could and ran toward First Mate Froggo to tell everyone that there was a panda with a bamboo sword guarding the tree house.

First Mate Froggo did as Capy Capy Capybara had told him to and warned everyone. Capy Capy Capybara noticed that the panda was about to hit Captain Knails Knusty, so he sprinted towards her and started attacking the panda while Captain Knails Knusty called for help. First Mate Froggo looked on at the fight and saw that Capy Capy Capybara was starting to grow very tired. He decided it was up to him to help the capybara, as the others had their own battles to deal with.

First Mate Froggo had done his research on specially trained pandas, and he now knew that pandas were obsessed with their hairstyles. If their hairstyle changed even in the slightest way, they would rush to the salon to get it redone. With this in mind, First Mate Froggo grabbed his own cutlass and gave the poor panda a mullet-styled haircut.

The panda was horrified and flew away to the Hair Salon Island not that far away. He screamed at the top of his voice, "OH NO!! My luscious locks are ruined!"

First Mate Froggo and Captain Knails Knusty turned their attention back to the crew only to see Pirate Pearl in a wrangle with the relentless Bearded Barry. Pirate Pearl was working her "Clamagic" on the unsuspecting Barry. Froggo and Knusty had never seen anything like it. Pirate Pearl whipped a shiny clam out of her pocket and whispered a secret message to the pearls inside it. The clam started shooting pearls like a machine gun at Bearded Barry. Almost blinded by the onslaught, Barry slumped to his knees, and the *Boberiño* crew knew victory was theirs

The crew jumped back on their ship and set sail again for the treasure. After what seemed like an eternity at sea, *Boberiño II* pulled up to a mysterious island off the coast of the Federated States of Micronesia.

The island had dark green grass, and in the middle there was a gloomy forest of dark oak trees. The crew were tired after days of travelling, so they decided it would be the perfect time to set up camp. After a couple of hours of scouting the island, the crew heard faint music coming from a dark and murky cave. Initially the crew decided not to go into the cave, but at that moment it started raining, so they swiftly escaped inside. As they went further into the cave, the music started getting louder and louder and LOUDER! Until they saw some lights. What they saw next would change everything...

A platform raised up before them. Curious to see what it was, First Mate Froggo and Pirate Pearl pushed their way to front of the crew for a closer look. They stepped onto the glowing platform and got prepared to dance. Suddenly two big red buttons rose from the ground. Out of curiosity they both pressed the buttons. Then a little coconut guy rolled into the room, and he said, "Get ready to dance." The little coconut guy started to sing, "I like to move it move it." Then he did a little boogie, and Pirate Pearl copied him.

First Mate Froggo had other plans, however. He tried to steal the coconut guy's funky glasses. What he did not know was that the coconut guy was a qualified martial arts master, and he karate chopped First Mate Froggo to the ground.

"Congrats!" said the coconut guy, handing a golden key to Pirate Pearl.

She walked over to the door on the other side of the platform and slowly turned the key to open the door. First Mate Froggo followed Pirate Pearl into a darkened room where a golden box of treasure lay on a lush red carpet. The pirates grabbed their riches and made a speedy exit.

The victorious crew trooped back to the ship with their shiny new riches in hand. They jumped aboard *Boberiño II*, eager to hand their booty back to Pirate King Grrrhooley. A wave of happiness washed over the triumphant crew as they relished in the fact that their quest was almost over.

Boberiño II set its course for Bruntsfield Bay. The crew left the Federated States of Micronesia singing raucously and revelling in their success.

They speedily returned to Pirate Bay and gave the treasure to Pirate King Grrrhooley, who was very pleased with their work.

22

ALL THE TREASURES, FINALLY, UNITED!

Success! The Bruntsfield Pirates had gathered their treasure chests into the assembly hall.

Each class captain stood by their gather bounty, waiting for Pirate King Grrrhooley to give the word.

With a wave of his cutlass, the Pirate King bellowed, "Open 'em up!"

The captains complied, but instead of seeing gold or jewels or cryptocurrency of any kind, they were met with a treasure far more valuable...

For you see, each chest contained a melodic word or two that poured out of them, singing this glorious shanty:

Letters make words...
Words make stories...
And through story, be written or told,
the beauty and diversity of the world
becomes available for all to behold!

A huge THANK YOU to the LOCAL BUSINESSES who helped fund this book!

- McLarens on the Corner
- Eye Surgeons of Edinburgh
- Viewforth Eyecare
- Montpeliers Bruntsfield (EST. 92)
- The Edinburgh Bookshop
- Ace Property Management & Sales
- 181 Delicatessen (ESTD. 2014)
- McDougall McQueen solicitors & estate agents
- Sean Murphy Dental Care
- Halibut and Herring
- Cuckoo's Bakery
- Bowerbird Antiques
- Snapdragon Edinburgh — botanically inspired
- W.M. Christie Family Butcher
- Thorne Records

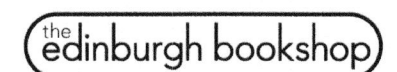

Wat's your Pirate story? Use these next pages to write your own story in this book.

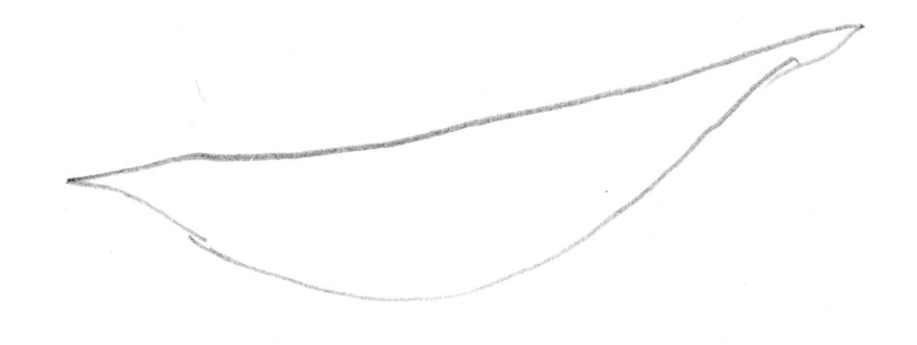

Printed in Great Britain
by Amazon